THE
CHURCH
THAT
REFUSED
TO DIE

D0807904

ROGER L. FREDRIKSON pastored the First Baptist Church of Wichita, Kansas—the setting for this book—from 1975 to 1987. His ministry has spanned more than four decades and has taken him into a variety of leadership positions in community and ministerial associations, including the presidency of his denomination.

Since 1987, Dr. Fredrikson has been involved in church renewal ministries in North America and Europe and is in high demand as a speaker and retreat leader. He is the author of three previous books.

THE
CHURCH
THAT
REFUSED
TO DIE

ROGER L. FREDRIKSON

VICTOR BOOKS®

A DIVISION OF SCRIPTURE PRESS PUBLICATIONS INC.
USA CANADA ENGLAND

Unless otherwise noted, Scripture quotations are from the *Revised Standard Version of the Bible,* © 1946, 1952, 1971, 1973. Other quotations are from the *King James Version* (KJV), and *The Living Bible* (TLB), © 1971, Tyndale House Publishers, Wheaton, Illinois 60189. Used by permission.

Library of Congress Cataloging-in-Publication Data

Fredrikson, Roger L.
 The church that refused to die / Roger L. Fredrikson.
  p. cm.
 Includes bibliographical references.
 ISBN 0-89693-257-5
 1. First Baptist Church (Wichita, Kan.) 2. Fredrikson,
Roger L.
 3. Wichita (Kan.) — Church history. I. Title
 BX6480.W463F74 1991
 286'.178186 — dc20   90-19293
                CIP

2 3 4 5 6 7 8 9 10 Printing/Year 95 94 93 92 91

Contents

To our three children
Randy, Miriam, and Joel

and their mates
Elaine, Frank, and Jan

and their children
Joel and Benjamin,
Elizabeth and Sarah,
Levi and Jacob

creative, caring people
who have helped me understand
what the healing grace of God is all about

F o r e w o r d

Fifteen years ago I went to Sioux Falls, South Dakota, to lead an interchurch campaign. My expectations were many—that the crowds would be good, that the city would become aware of the compelling message of Christ, that hundreds would begin to follow Him in a new way. As I recall, many of those expectations were fulfilled.

There was also an unexpected boon—the friendship of Roger Fredrikson, a man who ever since has held a special place in my heart. Roger stood high in the esteem of people in Sioux Falls and it was easy to see why. He was an excellent leader, a nationally known leader, a fine preacher, and a creative communicator.

But what struck me most about Roger Fredrikson was that he was a friend, a man in whose presence I always felt more transparent, more open, more free, to truly be myself. I came to sense deeply the presence of Christ in him.

So when Roger and Ruth were called to Wichita, I walked through that change with them long distance, in conversation and in prayer. I was surprised, but not too much so, that he would leave a place where he could have stayed the rest of his life and been admired and useful. But it was like Roger and Ruth to launch into a new adventure at an age when many people would be thinking of pulling back.

When I first visited the large, beautiful First Baptist sanctuary in Wichita and saw a handful of people there, I understood something of the faith and hope that it took for this move. But that venture on their part was met by a similar commitment from the people of this historic downtown church. The result is told in *The Church That Refused To Die,* a book I hope will be widely read.

The message of God's kingdom must be fleshed out in the ongoing life of local churches everywhere. While parachurch organizations fulfill very special needs, one of the best witnesses to the living Christ is a local congregation where people love and laugh and scrape their knees and get mad and forgive and pass Christ on to their city and their neighbors.

To take a living Christ into a needy America and into a needy world will take the planting of multiplied new congregations. And yet the renewal of the older churches is also a big part of the equation if God's plan is to be fully carried out.

As Roger Fredrikson likes to say, "God does new things, but He also makes old things new." Here is the story of how God helped a church become new. But the story is not just about Roger and Ruth or the people of First Baptist Wichita, special as they are. It is about Christ in them. That's what makes this story worth reading, because it means that what Jesus Christ did through them in Wichita, He can do through you and me anywhere.

Leighton Ford
Charlotte, North Carolina

Preface

Is it possible to speak of a church having a love affair? I hope so, for that is the best way I can describe what happened to First Baptist Church in Wichita, Kansas. Here is a church that knew the pain and humiliation and anger of schism, and was literally torn asunder. The remnant—about 400 out of what had once been over 4,000—were both uncertain and hopeful, wondering if the church had a future. Meeting in a huge, gray building that had been declared "theirs" by the Kansas Supreme Court, the church stood like a brooding sentinel at the heart of the city at Second and Broadway. Among the remnant were brave, expectant ones waiting on the Lord, believing He still had a mission for "Old First." And their prayers were answered.

The Lord had to drag me to Wichita. My wife, Ruth, knew we were to go there long before I did. Why should we leave Sioux Falls when we were having the time of our lives with an exciting congregation willing to take on almost any challenge that came down the pike? But I could not run away from the urgent, honest call for help which came from the people in Wichita—even though I kept trying. They did not soften the challenge: "We have a huge building and lots of problems. But we believe with the right leadership God has a ministry for us in this city." In the end that became the claim of the Lord on my life. And my "Yes" to that call became the most exhilarating, humbling, costly, at times exasperating — but also joyous — experience of my entire pastoral ministry. Literally a love affair with the Lord, among those people and for that city.

It was our first leaders' retreat in the fall of 1975 that we came on some strong words which became for us a specific promise. Spoken in times of desperate hopelessness both in the prophecy of Isaiah and the Revelation of John, "Behold, I am making all things new." What a word! Surely any work of renewal among us would be the Lord's doing, a gift like gentle rain falling on parched ground, given to us in the mystery of His sovereign grace, not through our clever schemes or anxious efforts, however sincere. We seized on that as our theme and hope.

And that is exactly what He began to do — renew us! Not quickly — He has His own timetable — but in quiet, almost imperceptible ways. There came a day when we seemed to know deep down He was working in this old, historic church. That gentle rain of healing, forgiving love was falling on fertile soil. There were small signs. Instead of people hurrying home in silence immediately after the services, they were lingering, visiting, and now and then praying with each other. They were wanting to cling to the fellowship as long as possible. And there was laughter once again — holy, joyous laughter. Strangers were being welcomed as friends. In Henri Nouwen's phrase, we were moving "from hostility to hospitality." Then one Sunday Billymae Marts, a grand, longtime member, summed it all up as she quietly greeted me after the service, "Pastor, it's different than it used to be. There hasn't been this much love around here in a long time." I could only praise the One who was sharing this gift with us.

So this is a story I have been compelled to tell, not to glorify this particular church, but to rejoice in our Lord's faithfulness. And to share my passionate conviction that He is far more eager to renew and empower the institutional church than we realize, even though it may be "out of focus," often whoring after other gods, suffering from a tentativeness and a loss of spiritual nerve. But Christ who loves the church and has given Himself for it is calling His people back to Himself. He purposes to use a chastened, cleansed, obedient church as His channel of redemption and hope, and to fill it with "the fullness of Himself."

This story is told to encourage other churches. New life can come! God's arm is not shortened. He can still do mighty things through ordinary people in situations that are hard and contrary. We can move from a survival mentality to vision; broken relationships can be healed; discouragement can give way to joy in the morning. Many congregations have suffered too long from unbelief and self-pity, constantly focusing on their problems rather than laying hold on the vast resources of the Father's storehouse. The Spirit does not visit us with renewing grace and vision because we worry and strain and push. His coming to quicken us is a gift given to those who pray and wait, who repent and receive, and then obey!

I have written quite specifically and autobiographically, believing we need to share what we are learning. I hope that my readers will move out from old institutional patterns and past failures into new adventures. A vision may come which seems wild and crazy and impossible. But before you dismiss it, talk it over with other people and pray about it. It could be the nudge of the Spirit.

I have written in snatches in all too infrequent moments. On planes and in airports, in pastors' homes and motels, as Ruth and I have moved about sharing in renewal conferences, but also in times of quiet in my small study in Sioux Falls as well as at our cabin on Lobster Lake in Minnesota.

There is no way I can thank that wonderful host of people who have allowed me to use their names. You do not know them but they are forgiven sinners, fellow saints, like those the Apostle Paul lists with such intimate tenderness in his letters. They are at the heart of this story, representative of those ministers we call the laity, the people of God.

Nor can I adequately thank my wife and friend, Ruth, an encourager and companion and lover for more than forty-five years. She typed the first rough draft, one of the few people who can decipher my scrawl. And she periodically asked as I was laboring over every word—sometimes painfully, but more often eagerly—"How is it coming?" And with that I know came her prayers.

And then LeeDel Howard carefully typed, refined, and re-typed whatever was sent her. As my faithful secretary all through the Wichita years, she quietly and efficiently kept a hundred details in order so the mission could be accomplished. She knows the inside of the story. I can never repay her! I salute her! She is now an administrative secretary at the American Baptist Assembly at Green Lake.

And thanks to a patient, long-suffering, but adventuresome staff who are very much a part of the story. Often they had to pick up the pieces. They know all about the failures as well as the accomplishments!

And special thanks to a dear friend and encourager, Edith Coe, who has run down all kinds of facts and material so that I could tell the story as accurately as possible. She has also obtained the permission of many people to use their names.

Years ago at the U.S. Congress on Evangelism in Minneapolis I came to know Leighton Ford better in a friendly, heart-to-heart conversation. It was an unexpected visit over dinner. We spoke of the meaning of biblical authority for our day, of these dangerous times so filled with crucial opportunity, and of the costly relational way in which the Gospel must be shared in this age if we are to get a hearing. Since then Leighton has been a close, trusted friend who has touched my life in more ways than he realizes, often strengthening and encouraging me in times of need and decision. I thank him for graciously agreeing to write the foreword.

Roger Fredrikson
Sioux Falls, South Dakota
1991

Chapter One

The Reluctant Servant

*"Then the word of the Lord came to
Jonah the second time." Jonah 3:1*

When I answered the phone that December evening in 1974, it took a minute or two to place the person calling. She identified herself as Edith Clemmons Coe from Wichita, Kansas. Then I remembered. She was that enthusiastic YWCA representative who was part of our U.S.A. delegation to the second World Conference of Christian Youth. That was in Oslo, Norway in 1947—the first international church conference after World War II. An unforgettable experience for all of us!

After a bit of reminiscing, Edith got down to business. She had just come from a meeting of the Pulpit Committee of the First Baptist Church. Before adjourning for the Christmas holidays, they had given her permission to call me with a kind of "It probably won't do any good, but go ahead and call anyway" attitude. The committee had already been down so many dead-end streets.

I was taken aback somewhat when Edith asked, "How would you like to add one more star to your well-filled crown?" I wasn't at all certain I had won any stars and sometimes wondered if I even had a crown. But I drew a deep breath. "What do you mean by that?"

"We want you to consider coming to be our pastor at First

Baptist." Before I could give her a "No, I don't really think I'm interested" response as kindly as possible, she became more specific. "My husband, John, and I will be on our way to Israel via Chicago in January, and we could easily come through Sioux Falls. We would like to stop by and visit with you and Ruth."

I wondered. Did I want to get involved in any kind of discussion with the Wichita church? I was somewhat aware of the trouble it had been through—once an aggressive congregation of more than 4,000 members, noted for its evangelistic and missionary zeal, involved in a building program hardly keeping pace with its growth. But then a spirit of misunderstanding had crept in among the members. Suspicions of doctrinal carelessness among the leaders of the American Baptist Convention, with which the church was affiliated, as well as charges of political involvement by the National Council of Churches, were repeatedly voiced by a particular group.

And as people divided up sides, they became increasingly unwilling to listen to one another. Finally there had been a painful rupture and a prolonged struggle in the Kansas courts to determine which group had rightful title to the building. Now instead of one congregation there were two—First Baptist, an American Baptist Church, and Metropolitan Baptist, which eventually became a Southern Baptist Church and splintered into a third group, an independent Baptist church called Beth-Eden. This whole episode had been given wide publicity in both church and secular press.

Edith was calling that night in behalf of the minority, the American Baptist congregation which had finally been given possession of the building. This committed remnant hoped God had a brighter, more hopeful future for them.

In spite of my misgivings, I could not bring myself to tell Edith and John Coe we were not willing to have them come by and visit us. At least we would hear their story and perhaps encourage them a bit. However, I did not have the slightest interest in even considering becoming their pastor. After almost sixteen years in Sioux Falls, we still had too many exciting things going on to even think of leaving. The Firehouse, a unique Christian coffeehouse which our church had gotten into "with both feet," was jumping with life every evening from eight to midnight. In a city filled with single adults and all kinds of students, more than 20,000 of them were coming through our doors every year. The Glory House, a halfway house for men coming out of the state penitentiary, which had been launched on a hope and a prayer by our church, was having a redemptive impact beyond our wildest dreams. And we had just begun a Crisis and Help Ministry centered in the church building—a rather unusual venture for a suburban congregation. Sixty-six of our people had signed up on the first call for volunteers. Best of all, people were coming to confess Christ in almost every service of worship. And we were just getting underway in celebrating our centennial.

My feelings of curiosity about the Wichita church must have outrun my hesitation, for I did agree with Edith on a date for their visit, Sunday, January 12. . . . "And then we can go out for lunch and a visit after our eleven o'clock service."

On January 11 the snows came. What began so gently and beautifully became a raging blizzard. *The Argus-Leader,* our local newspaper, reported winds gusting up to eighty miles an hour with the windchill temperature getting down to sixty-two degrees below zero. And this continued hour after hour.

It was with some sense of relief that I said to Ruth, "Well, now at least we won't have to concern ourselves with the Coe visit." I spoke too soon, for just then the phone rang. It was John and Edith calling from Sioux City, seventy miles to the south. I could hardly believe they had gotten that far. They were wondering if we would be having services the next day. "Of course," I replied somewhat self-righteously. "We never cancel our morning worship services. We're on the radio, which means we always have a great homebound congregation whenever the weather is bad. A great opportunity for us, regardless of who shows up in the sanctuary. But for heaven's sake, stay where you are. There is no point in risking your necks. The State Patrol is insisting that everyone stay off all the roads." But I had no idea how tenacious and resourceful the Coes could be. John's only reply was, "We'll see you tomorrow." I was certain that was impossible.

On the morrow I called on our good friend Evans Nord for help. He had said, "If there's ever anything I can do for the good of the cause just give me a call." I remembered he had a four-wheel-drive Bronco, and this was the time to find out if he would really make good on his offer. He came through with flying colors. "I'll be right there." Our church staff was delivered to the church door on time by this eager chauffeur.

Traffic was at a standstill everywhere. Eight deaths had already been reported and at least 3,000 head of cattle had frozen in the storm—the worst since the great blizzard of 1880. We had gotten word to four local radio stations that the services at First Baptist would go on as usual. Perhaps there was some fleshly pride in letting the community know we were in business. One of the radio announcers did comment when he received our call, "That's the first good news I've heard all day." Our regular snow crew cleared the church parking lot, which prompted one of our friendly critics to comment, "Those crazy Baptists. No one can get to church, but they have the parking lot cleared."

But some people did get to church. Fifty or so for the first service—not our usual 8:30 crowd, many of them people from the neighborhood. Most had walked, congratulating one another they had made it to church. That spirit carried over into our worship as we sang, praised God, and prayed for those caught in the pain and destruction of the storm. When I stood up to read the Scripture, which had been chosen months earlier, I was overwhelmed by the timeliness of the words: "God is our refuge and strength, a very present help in trouble. Therefore we will not fear though the earth should change, though the mountains shake in the heart of the sea; though its waters roar and foam, though the mountains tremble with its tumult" (Psalm 46:1-3). The Lord had certainly written the script for the day!

Between services we drank coffee and wondered who would show up for the next service. I could not help thinking about the Coes, hoping they had given up or turned back, and that they hadn't ended up in the ditch! We were delighted when about 225 hardy souls (another interesting crowd) came stomping in sharing talk of the storm. Victor Balla, our innovative associate pastor, had recruited thirty courageous folks to serve as our choir. I remember laughingly suggesting that perhaps we should have a special prayer for these hastily gathered songsters. The Lord certainly heard whatever prayer was offered, because they sang "All Hail the Power of Jesus' Name" with unexpected power and harmony.

As we were singing our first hymn John and Edith walked in, exuding a quiet spirit of triumph. They smiled and nodded as if to say, "We told you we'd be here." I could only stare back, wondering how they did it.

I have heard the Coes explain a half dozen times how they made the journey from Sioux City to Sioux Falls—through single-lane traffic on desperately slippery Interstate 29, with cattle crossing the fences on the rocklike snow and running crazily along the highway, and their passing scores of stalled and stranded cars. But I am not quite certain to this day I understand how they managed to cover those seventy miles. It was almost like the Children of Israel crossing the Red Sea on dry ground, except that this time it was Interstate 29 from Sioux City to Sioux Falls.

However, I believe now the courageous, almost foolhardy determination displayed by John and Edith in making that trip was a factor in our decision finally to heed the call and move to Wichita. We were to discover when we got to Wichita that these two lived on the edge of adventure. Their drive on frozen roads was no exception. They enjoyed tackling new things, like encouraging the church to buy the property next door when the mortuary standing there burned down—to double our parking space; like entertaining the whole church for a great family picnic on their farm early each fall, deep-frying 100 chickens in huge black pots to feed the hungry multitude; or encouraging the pastor to go ahead on some new untried church venture. How often in the years to come I was to thank God for their warm support.

After the service that snowy Sunday in Sioux Falls, we found a restaurant open for business and over lunch heard the Coes state their case for the Wichita church. Yes, the people had become discouraged. The pulpit committee had almost come to the end of its rope. After more than two years without a regular pastor and a number of turndowns from prospects, they were wondering now if anyone was willing to come and lead them. They had a huge building and a small congregation still working at paying off the debt. John estimated there were perhaps 400 regular members. And this congregation was made up mostly of older folks, although a few younger couples had dared join.

But there was also hope! A stalwart band who had been through the fire still stubbornly believed God had a ministry for them and they had a longing for spiritual renewal. As John put it, "We have lots of problems and a big building, but we believe with the right leadership and the Lord's help we can have a great ministry."

And Ruth and I were as honest with them. We were perfectly happy in Sioux Falls and deeply committed to that ministry which was increasingly touching the whole city. The Coes were gently persistent. How did we know the Lord wanted us to stay in Sioux Falls, if we weren't at least willing to come down and check out their situation? Surely we could do this without making any commitment. Would we join them for breakfast and let them know if we could work out a visit to Wichita? This we agreed to do, somewhat reluctantly.

John and Edith returned for our evening service, the "People's Service." A time of informal song, sharing, and prayer, with a scriptural teaching and much participation. Surprisingly, 196 enthusiastic people showed up in the bitter cold. South Dakotans are a strange breed, actually enjoying the challenge of what ordinary people call "terrible weather." That night "There's a sweet, sweet Spirit in this place" was sung with special meaning. At the conclusion, after a simple message from Ephesians, four people came forward—a young couple to accept Christ and two students to join our church.

After the service John was really excited. "This has been a tremendous experience. Why, I believe eighty percent of the folks here tonight were young people. You'd be crazy to leave this." I could only respond, "John, I have no intention of leaving this. There's too much going on. For example, there were converted ex-druggers with us tonight, who have come to Christ by way of The Firehouse. And all kinds of students from Sioux Falls and Augustana Colleges are very much a part of our congregational life. We have prayerfully drawn together a creative church staff which is just now becoming a team. And there's a beautiful spirit of unity and caring among our people. I don't think anything could drag us away."

I was a bit late for our breakfast date. Early that morning I had been called about an Augustana College student who had frozen to death with his buddy. The two had foolishly left their stalled VW east of town on their way to Minnesota and had gotten lost in the blinding snowstorm. They were found huddled in a ditch in their sleeping bags. So I found it difficult to concentrate on our conversation with the Coes over bacon and eggs.

To this day I cannot humanly explain why Ruth and I agreed to visit Wichita on March 12. The Coes would be back from their trip to Israel, and apparently that date seemed "safely removed." I thought our visit might give these dear people a lift, and possibly we could suggest a name or two of potential pastors. So the Coes went on their way, and Ruth and I put the whole matter to rest—at least for the time being!

But March 12 came sooner than we expected and as we journeyed to Wichita I wondered uneasily, "Why are we doing this anyhow?" It really seemed an unnecessary trip. We were met at the airport by Hal and Zattie Moody—an older, courageous couple who had weathered all the storms at the church, faithfully standing by their posts. Hal was on the pulpit committee and had served as church treasurer for years. And Zattie, a gifted Sunday School teacher, let us know immediately as we greeted one another, "You pronounce my name Zăttie, not Zāttie."

They took us to Brown's Cafeteria, a busy noontime eating place a block from the church, to meet with the committee. We first met Ed Friesen, their chairman, a public school administrator who had served half a dozen Wichita elementary and junior high schools as a principal with distinction over a thirty-year period. He was later inducted into the Kansas Teacher's Hall of Fame. Ed was a man of deep conviction and rare integrity, qualities he had brought with him from his Mennonite background. There was Helen McAfee, an outgoing, caring woman, recently retired from the Internal Revenue Service, now serving as the church secretary. And Rod Busey, a quiet, thoughtful attorney who was looked upon as the "constitutional expert" of the church. He was frequently joshed good-naturedly for showing up late at meetings, but he always knew what was going on.

Alan Criddlebaugh, the youngest member of the committee, was stationed at McConnell Air Force Base. Then there was Kenneth Ellsworth, a son of the church, who had served as a pastor in a number of places in Kansas before becoming the administrator of Prairie Homestead, a retirement community launched mainly through the investment and influence of people in First Baptist. George Morgan, an enthusiastic layman who never hesitated to speak his mind, recently retired from an executive position with Sears, had been asked to sit in with the committee, possibly to reinforce the whole procedure.

These, along with Edith Coe and Hal Moody, made quite a group. It was obvious they had been through some disappointing times over the last several months, following up one lead after another trying to find the right man. Most recently a pastor whom they fully expected would come had refused at the last moment, because the call extended was two votes shy of being unanimous. Little wonder they seemed somewhat nervous about our visit.

Our gathering was not exactly a white linen tablecloth affair—just a simple soup and sandwich luncheon in a side room. I couldn't help thinking, "There is something appealing about this unadorned, honest approach. No one is out to impress anyone. It fits the situation." How unlike some pulpit committees that go to great lengths in elegant eating establishments to "sell" the prospective pastor.

And the conversation was as honest as the surroundings. They were up-front in speaking of their history and struggle as a church. Their message was the same as we had heard from the Coes—"We've got lots of problems and a big building, but we believe with the right kind of leadership God has a great future for this congregation."

I tried to respond in like manner. We had really come to visit with them quite reluctantly because we were still challenged by our ministry in Sioux Falls, and we were not there to play games with them. Still, it would help to get some answers.

- How many active, committed members did they still have?
- Were they willing to enter into a relational style of ministry?
- Would they be open to new forms of ministry to reach the city?
- Were they willing to make the spiritual and financial sacrifice to move into God's future?
- How much did they still owe on the building?
- Would they be willing to open the building in an expanded ministry?

Their answers were strong and positive. These people were eager for the church to move forward.

Of course, they eventually got to the big question. Would Ruth and I seriously consider coming to serve their church as pastor? Even though I said, "That is the least we could do," I really assumed we had done the "serious considering" already. Intriguing as this visit was turning out to be, I was certain God wasn't finished with us in Sioux Falls. So, I thought that in a couple of weeks we would call and thank them for their gracious kindness and say, "We have thought over your kind invitation but cannot accept it. But we surely will remember you in prayer." Our meeting concluded with prayer and we moved toward the church to take a look at the "big building."

As we entered the church, an imposing gray structure standing at Second and Broadway, we had an unexpected encounter with Jean Gragg—or was it planned? She was a gracious businesswoman, named one of the "uncommon citizens" of the community by the Chamber of Commerce, and deeply committed to the church through thick and thin. She was also one of the most optimistic and generous people I have ever met. After some pleasantries she quietly whispered, "I believe you should come. If you do, we'll love you to pieces." Her words linger to this day. We later discovered she was a woman of her word.

We moved through the south educational building first, five stories of Sunday School classrooms, nurseries, and staff offices with a fellowship hall and kitchen in the basement. This building had been completed in 1957. I was a bit overwhelmed when we visited the pastor's study, finished in beautiful mahogany and lined with bookshelves. It seemed the center of "ecclesiastical power," and I wondered how any poor, needy soul would dare climb the stairs with the marble-lined walls to enter that place on the second floor.

Then we walked into the majestic, stately sanctuary with its lofty vaulted ceiling, its 1,802 individual red opera seats, and the beautiful rose windows at either end—Christ and the Apostles high above the baptistry, and The Word and the Prophets at the back of the balcony. W.C. Coleman, famed for the Coleman lantern and founder of the company that bore his name, had planned this place of worship after visiting church buildings all over the country. It was obvious the influence of this truly great Christian statesman was still felt throughout the congregation twenty years after his death. The cornerstone for this building had been laid in 1949 and the building was dedicated with great joy on September 10, 1950.

We then moved into the old north building, dating back to 1928, a four-story center of activity with more classrooms, a gymnasium, a parlor, and chapel. I remember wondering if these people would be willing to update and beautify this building and what the cost of utilities and upkeep might be and thinking, "There is no way any church can justify such a building if it is used only one or two days a week."

That evening before leaving town we had dinner with Ray Parry, a warmhearted brother I had known for years. The few months he expected to serve First Baptist as interim pastor had stretched beyond two years. He was weary in well-doing and eager to get home to his beloved Colorado.

Ray's contagious, optimistic spirit had given a lift to the congregation. He took great delight in throwing parties of one kind or another. The special gourmet desserts served in his apartment or the Easter evening celebration around the pool at the Royale, a classy downtown motel, or the boisterous mother-daughter banquet with Helen McAfee sashaying in as "Dolly" will never be forgotten. He helped the people understand again that getting involved with Jesus can be a joyous affair.

Over our crepes that evening we had a refreshingly frank conversation. Ray voiced surprise that we had come to visit with the committee. "Are you really serious? I don't see how you could even think of leaving Sioux Falls. I have great memories of that church from student days." I assured him we had not come to play games. But how could we know for certain we were to stay on in Sioux Falls, if we were unwilling to consider anything else? After all, I had no corner on knowing the will of God. But now, even though we had heard the deeply moving cry for help voiced by these Wichita folks, I was still certain there was no way we could contemplate leaving Sioux Falls. There were simply too many ties there and too many unfulfilled dreams.

Then I tried to turn it back on Ray. "These people really love you. You've given them tremendous encouragement and new hope. You're the one who should become their permanent pastor." "No way," was his immediate answer. "These are wonderful people and I've had a great time with them, but I'm going back to Colorado. I've done all I can do. And there's that building. I could never live with that building. I tried to convince them they should sell it and move out nearer the people, but most of them stubbornly insist they belong downtown!" Then he shared some of the fun times but also heartaches he had passed through with them, and we prayed and said good-bye.

As we left town pondering all that had taken place, Ruth broke the silence. "I find this kind of exciting." I could hardly believe my ears. Ruth has always been the one who gladly tended the home fires, rejoicing in our ministry together, but not one for pulling up roots. I was the one who was always running off some place, ever since youth fellowship days, trying to save the world, even traveling well over 100,000 miles the year I served as the president of our convention. I could only respond, "You don't mean to tell me you'd want to live in Wichita, Kansas, of all places. Why it's so flat and the wind blows and it can get terribly hot—and there's that building!"

Then she really surprised me. "I wonder if we aren't losing our sense of pilgrimage in Sioux Falls." I found myself feeling defensive, almost wanting to say, "You let me handle this!" Yet she wasn't being argumentative, only stating her honest convictions. I tried to brush her off by saying, "Well, we'll have to think and pray about this, but I really don't believe our work in Sioux Falls is finished." So we drove on in silence, but the issue was far from closed.

The next Sunday during dinner, Ruth said a rather strange thing. "I could hardly see anyone today during worship and I had an awful time trying to sing the words of the choir anthem." When I asked, "Why? Are you having trouble with your eyes?" she caught me completely off-guard. "No, my eyes kept filling with tears because I know we're not going to be here long and I love these dear people like my own family." I tried to hide my perplexity and irritation. What kind of pressure was this woman trying to put on me? What did she know that I didn't? I was the pastor. Wasn't I supposed to have a special way of perceiving the will of God? And I didn't seem to be getting the same message she was.

How wrong I was! For now the struggle I had not anticipated began. I could not bring myself to call Ed Friesen in Wichita in a couple of weeks, as I had promised, to tell him, "Sorry, but you'd better look elsewhere." I would tell myself, "I'll call him tomorrow," but the days became weeks. Finally I did call asking for a bit more time and Ed's answer was, "Take all the time you need. We've waited a long time and a few more days won't make that much difference."

I could not shake that call for help: "We've got lots of problems and a big building, but with the right leadership we believe great things can happen for the Lord." One day I would find myself asking, "Am I the 'right leadership,' Lord? Is Wichita a call from You? Something You are asking me to do?" But the next day I would assure myself, "This is where we belong. The Lord has much unfinished business all around us — the development of a retreat center, the strengthening of the Crisis and Help Ministry, and so much more! And look at the strong, gifted staff we've finally brought together. Surely they need my pastoral guidance and support." Then I would seem to hear another voice, "Would you give it all up for Me?" It was a miserable time of indecisiveness and uncertainty.

How often we speak almost glibly and easily of "knowing God's will" as if it were dropped down on stone tablets or came by opening the Bible at random and pointing to a particular verse. But do we not come to understand His marching orders best in times of tension and wrestling and of waiting? Jacob at the brook of Jabbok? Moses at the burning bush? Jeremiah at the potter's wheel? Jesus in the wilderness? Paul waiting in blindness?

During this time I needed support—emotional and spiritual. And I turned to two trusted colleagues—Ed Novak, pastor of First Lutheran, and Monsignor Louis Delahoyde of the Catholic Chancery Office. Strange for a Baptist pastor? Not at all. For several years the three of us had participated in a unique TV talk show called "The Open Door" on Channel 11. Each Saturday afternoon at 4:30 we would sit down together around a table with a coffeepot and three cups—which really tested Louis Delahoyde's ecumenical spirit, for he was not much of a coffee fan. At least he toyed with the cup. And then the three of us would engage in a frank, lively conversation—although now and then it could drag—on any given topic that was "hot" for one of us at the time: "Does the institutional church have a future?" "How can we really know we're forgiven?" "How can we best understand and help the Native Americans?" "Why do Baptists make so much over water?" "What is the meaning of the Roman Catholic confessional?" We never seemed to run out of things to talk about. And never ceased being amazed how all kinds of people seemed delighted that the three of us could visit with one another as friends.

Of course, there was also the other kind of response, like on the day when we stopped for a snack in Chamberlain on our way home from western South Dakota. When I stepped into the bar to pay the bill at the only cash register open for business I was addressed by a gentleman who was obviously somewhat inebriated. "Say, aren't you one of those fellows on television?" When I couldn't deny it he went on, "Well, you've set religion back thirty years." Now I was curious, "How can that be?" He seemed eager to let me know. "I used to give fifty dollars a year to the church before I started watching you fellows; now I give fifteen." This announcement was made to all those gathered in the place. I thought it best not to continue that conversation. But this was only one kind of reaction. Most were friendly and affirming. And occasionally there was even an urgent call for help.

Through all those years—we had recently celebrated our

tenth anniversary—we came to love and respect one another. So one day I opened my heart to these two men and shared my struggle and ambivalence about the Wichita situation. And these brothers were more than eager to join me in prayer.

Two weeks later when we had finished taping another show, Pastor Novak asked, "Well, have you made a decision about that Wichita church?" "Yes, thank God that's all settled," I replied. "I believe the marvelous staff meeting this morning was really a sign from the Lord that we're to stay here! We had a beautiful spirit of unity as we talked about our hopes for the future of the church. It was a time of renewed expectations." Both men graciously assured me it would be a joy to continue our relationship. I could only thank them for their loving support as we started to leave.

But as we neared our cars Monsignor Delahoyde hesitated for a moment, then dropped it on me oh so gently, "Of course, I'm glad you're staying. Our camaraderie, which I have truly enjoyed, can continue. But I cannot forget how you spoke about that Wichita opportunity a couple of weeks ago, wondering if you weren't being called to cast your lot with those people for the next ten years or so, giving them and the Lord the best of your strength and hopes. That kind of abandon in ministry is in the finest tradition of Roman Catholic pastoral theology."

I don't think my friend Delahoyde knew the impact of what he was saying, but it came home like an arrow! I got into the car completely taken aback, unable to drive away for a time. First it was Ruth and now the Monsignor. Then I heard it clearly and distinctly—His voice! "That's My word to you." I was devastated. All my defenses had been stripped away. But still I argued, "Not from a Roman Catholic priest!" But He caught me again. "I'll speak to you any way I choose. If My word can be uttered through Balaam's ass, surely I can make My will known through a priest."

I drove to McKennan Hospital in a turmoil, struggling to give up what I thought was mine but had been His all the time. Here I was a so-called "successful pastor," pinned to the mat by a gracious, sovereign Lord whose ways are not our ways, who was asking that I capitulate again and turn it all over to Him. And I would never know peace until I did. I went in to make some calls at the hospital, not remembering who I saw or what I said.

Then home! Ruth greeted me warmly, "Welcome home, honey. What kind of a day has it been?" I could only reply, "Awful. I believe the worst day of my life. It started with an enthusiastic, hopeful staff meeting, so unusual I was certain it was a sign from the Lord that this is our place. And ended with a word that upset all my plans. And of all things it was a simple, almost off-handed thing Monsignor Delahoyde said. Something he had picked up in our conversation a couple of weeks ago. And he simply turned it back on me, not knowing how much was involved in what he was saying. But I know it was the unmistakable word of the Lord. He is calling us to give up this beloved church and community to strike out for Wichita. And, dear Ruth, you've known from the first this is what the Lord wanted."

Without a word she picked up a book she had been reading, *Something More* by Catherine Marshall, opened it and pointed to a chapter she had read that day entitled, "The Joy of Obedience." Then she turned to the end of the chapter which closes with these costly but liberating words, "So Abraham obeyed. He went out, not knowing whither he went."[1] We simply looked at each other, embraced, and our tears were mingled—the tears of surrender.

There was only one thing to do—call Ed Friesen in Wichita and tell him if the church still wanted us to come we would join them in the ministry there. His quiet "Hallelujah!" in response to that call was both a gift and an affirmation. It was then peace came. Now there could be no turning back. So Ed and I went on to make plans for our coming to visit with the whole congregation.

That evening Ruth and I had a strong inner prompting to go out and spend a bit of time with Merton and Pat Peterson, beloved friends and stalwart members of First Baptist. We had enjoyed many festive occasions at their home. But this was different. Merton, who had seemed in perfect health, was in the last stages of leukemia. In those closing days he had come home to be with his family in familiar surroundings. During this strange, dark time Merton and Pat had grown in grace. One could sense a luminous glow about them.

In the early stages of the disease, after coming home from the Mayo Clinic, Merton had pointedly asked, "Why haven't you preached more on the Psalms? I found tremendous encouragement in them these last days as I read one psalm after another, some of them over and over again." I could only accept this as an admonition from a fellow believer. So I too turned to these writings again to discover anew their lyrical beauty and power as I tried to share their meaning with our people. So contemporary, speaking to our deepest needs and estrangement, but also expressing our joys and gratitude.

On our way out to see the Petersons that night, we came to a high place overlooking the city. I stopped the car and looked back. A thousand lights glistened in the darkness of the early evening. I could not help but feel a stab of pain, and tried to choke down crying out, "This is my town. We belong to these people. Here's where our children have grown up and where we have invested sixteen years of our lives." Once again I wondered if we were making an awful mistake in leaving. Had the peace I had known earlier left me? I shook off the doubt and we drove on.

Our visit with the Petersons was very brief. Merton was in the grip of deadening pain, struggling for every breath. There was only a short greeting, a word of Scripture, and a prayer. And we left!

On our way home it struck me—Merton and Pat were letting go too! But theirs was the final act of surrender. The discovery of life in death, one releasing the other to begin the everlasting adventure in the Father's house.

But is this not what our Heavenly Father is always calling us to do? Give up the familiar for the greater plan, leave the security of the harbor for the risk of sailing in the deep. Has this not always been the story of God's people moving into new country by faith—the fishermen leaving their nets and their father? Paul crossing over from Troas to Macedonia? Chuck Colson giving up power and prestige to minister among the prisoners of our society? Millard Fuller letting go of his personal fortune and ambition to enlist an army of people in Habitat for Humanity to provide decent housing for the poor? We are always claimed by the grace of One who "though He was rich, yet for your sake He became poor, so that by His poverty you might become rich" (2 Corinthians 8:9).

Surely we could trust that One as we tried to obey Him in His calling us to Wichita, a place which now seemed so strange and distant. The Lord had quietly but decisively spoken to me through that brief but incredibly deep encounter with Merton and Pat. It was then that a strong, settled peace, "a peace which passes understanding," was given me which did not leave me during the weeks ahead, so full of emotional and spiritual demands.

On April 22 I journeyed to Wichita to meet with the congregation. On my way down, I could not help wondering, "Am I really doing the right thing?" So, between flights, I gave my longtime friend John Erickson a call from the Kansas City airport. When he discovered what I was up to, he insisted on coming out "so that we can talk it over and pray about it." My protests were to no avail. After all, his office was twenty miles from the airport and he was the national president of the Fellowship of Christian Athletes. His only response was, "What are friends for?" In a short time he was there, and the next precious moments of conversation and prayer will linger with me all my days. What a gift!

Later that afternoon, Ed Friesen and his wife, Thelma, welcomed me so graciously in their comfortable home that I felt I had known them all my life. They were obviously excited about the meeting that night, hoping it would go well. And I could not help wondering what was in store for me.

How can I ever forget walking into that well-filled fellowship hall to break bread and mingle with the people who were to become our spiritual family. I was deeply touched by the warmth of their greeting. A spirit of anticipation filled the place. But I could not help noticing all the gray heads, although I did spot a younger person here and there.

Ed Friesen was very kind in presenting me to the people as he explained some of our "negotiations," indicating I was open to serve as their pastor if they should call me. I responded by making it clear that I had not come to prove anything or to sell myself. But how could I let this new family know a bit of who I was and how I approached the ministry? I still have the notes I had scrawled on the back of a folder on the flight down. Convictions I had hammered out and struggled over in more than twenty years of serving two congregations.

- The authority of the Word of God under which the church must live.
- The power and freedom of a relational, caring way of life among God's people, often discovered best in small prayer groups drawn together for support and growth and outreach.
- Calling forth the gifts of the laity and equipping them for ministry.
- The church being Christ's servant people in the community.
- A flexible, mobile strategy in 'being all things to all people' in reaching them for Christ.
- An open agenda, allowing the Spirit to constantly renew a people and lead them into new places of service.
- The utter centrality of giving glory to God, the Father, Son, and Holy Spirit through lifting, authentic worship.

I assured these dear friends I had my peculiar foibles and great clay feet. Later they were to understand how true that was.

Well, it was all a bit overwhelming, but finally some questions were raised. "How would you start your ministry if you came?" "Tell us about your family." "Would you try to get a coffeehouse and a halfway house underway here as you have done in Sioux Falls?" "Do you really take a day off every week?" A wise, retired physician, Dr. Henry Loewen, asked, "When did you last have an electrocardiogram? It will take a strong heart to lead our church." He was not joking.

Then someone asked, "What do you plan to do now?" "I expect to go home and resign from the church in Sioux Falls this Sunday." I could sense that my answer caused something of a stir. I soon realized why. "We haven't even called you yet, and according to our constitution we have to post the name of any prospective pastor two weeks before the congregation votes to extend a call." That was not the first or last time I have caused constitution writers concern. I could only respond, "I have fought the battle and I know my ministry in Sioux Falls is finished. If this church should choose not to call me, I am certain the Lord has some ministry elsewhere." There was a bit of embarrassed laughter.

But in my heart of hearts, I knew the Lord had laid His hand on me, had claimed me for His ministry among these people in Wichita. That inner assurance of the Lord's calling ran deeper than any human vote, as important as that might be. I was to be renewed again and again by that certainty in times of discouragement and weakness in the years that followed. Just before that meeting came to a closing time of prayer, a younger woman stood up asking to be recognized and then almost shouted, "All I can say is Hallelujah!"

We drove out to the Friesen home where I was to spend the night, rejoicing and praising God. It really had been a "Hallelujah night."

I came home on Wednesday from that visit. Thursday Merton Peterson died. I got to the hospital to join Pat just as Merton breathed his last. His "homegoing" service was on Saturday—a glorious celebration of the Resurrection, mingled with the painful tears of separation—one of those times when it seemed Jesus danced in the aisles.

An hour after the service I met with our church council. One could feel they were wondering, "Why are we here?" "What's he up to now?" How could I break the news? There was no easy, correct way to let these trusted friends know we would be leaving for another place of ministry. I was emotionally drained and needed an extra measure of grace and strength, which came in prayer before I plunged ahead with the reason for this hastily called meeting. The needs of a struggling, broken congregation in Wichita, Kansas had become the call of the Lord for us. I could not turn aside from that claim, try as I would. So on the morrow I proposed to share this with all our people in worship and ask for their release and blessing! It was a heavy moment. Of course, there were questions and some tears, but also a quiet understanding. And I continued to experience that inner peace which can only be a gift of the Spirit.

The next morning I came to our worship services with that same sense of God's wondrous presence. Otherwise, I could never have faced that loving family and shared my personal struggle to be obedient. It was not a question of one congregation being better or more important than the other. Simply a matter of coming to the place where I could say "Yes" to the "Macedonian Call."

I have never believed we humans are in a position to vote on the call of God, but only to hear Him, affirm that call, and obey! So at the conclusion I asked the people who were willing to send us on our way with their blessing and prayers to stand. The quiet hush of that moment is with me to this day. Then people began to stand here and there until all were on their feet. And that in both services. It was a mighty benediction, an affirmation of the Lord leading.

Our oldest son, Randy, was with us that day in worship, mingling his tears and deep feelings with ours. After the second service he joined Ruth and me as we quietly slipped out during the closing hymn, "The Church's One Foundation Is Jesus Christ Her Lord." How fitting! I was delighted to learn later that a couple had come forward to give themselves to Christ in response to the invitation. The three of us journeyed south about thirty miles to Tolly's Restaurant for our Sunday dinner. As we broke bread and shared both in silence and conversation out of the deeps of our lives, I had an overwhelming sense of relief and gratitude. This was truly a sacramental meal for me.

And oh yes, the "official" call did come from the Wichita church, right on time, after the two-week notice. And it was unanimous—which surprised me a bit. I felt surely there might be some negative votes after that heavy introduction session we had been through.

Somehow we survived the farewells of the next few weeks. Those acts of kindness and tender words still linger with us. We struggled not to succumb to the sin of gluttony as we went from home to home partaking of one delicious meal after another. It was all part of the ritual of letting go and being sent on our way. We even managed to pull off a garage sale. How do you clean out all the unneeded stuff and lighten the load, after sixteen years in the same house? It was a major victory when I got our storeroom cleaned, discovering things I had forgotten we had.

In the midst of this the Sioux Falls congregation was celebrating 100 years of service and witness for the Lord. It was a week of very special events—a televised worship service; a picnic on the lawn; an old-timers' night when fifty-year members came in vintage cars; the weekend visit of Gus and Dorothy Hintz, beloved former pastor and wife who in earlier years had given extraordinary leadership to the church; and all climaxed by a joyous river baptism.

In those final days, as I was trying to pack several hundred books, I had an unexpected caller. A young man home from college, whom I scarcely knew, walked into the church study insisting he had to see me. He insisted he had something important to tell me. I could hardly contain my irritation, although I responded as pleasantly as possible. "You say what you must and I'll keep on working with the books." He had just come home from a conference of charismatic Lutherans held in Minneapolis. I wondered why reporting on that to me was so urgent. One of the speakers, he said, had chosen, "Behold, I am making all things new" as his text. Then he had gone on to point out that the Lord does not simply make new things, but takes all kinds of old things, tired people and dying churches, and unhealed situations, and makes them new.

By this time the young man had my attention. "David," I said, "I'm sorry I was so short and impatient with you. Please sit down. I believe you have a word from the Lord. And I really need to hear that right now." So we opened our hearts to one another, shared a bit, and had a beautiful time of prayer.

In almost twelve years in Wichita, I lived in the assurance and hope of those words. And I watched in wonder as He fulfilled His promise, "making all things new."

Where Does Renewal Start?

It starts with you! Right where you are—in the kitchen or the classroom, on a construction crew or in a retirement home, and often in the church. There is a call that comes, sometimes very loudly and clearly, but at other times faintly and almost indistinctly. But it is always personal, never general. "Come, follow Me," was spoken to certain men who were fishing.

A caring friend shares a vision with me or I hear the cry of an aching need. But however the message comes, I know I have been confronted and called. Now I become restless, ill at ease, even rebellious. "Surely that can't mean me. I could never do that." But I cannot shake it. For now I know the Lord is dealing with me. I must either say yes or run—obey or reject!

For me it was John and Edith Coe whose kind, challenging words haunted me, then dear Ruth who seemed so certain the Lord was speaking to us, and then that quiet word from

Monsignor Delahoyde. Do you suppose the Lord is trying to say something to you through a Sunday School teacher, a pastor, a wise friend, or even through someone completely unexpected—a skeptic taunting you or an alcoholic crying out for help? Are you listening?

The Lord isn't at all impressed with position or status. He knows who He needs and how that person can serve Him. After all, He once did His work through a prostitute named Rahab and harnessed a hotheaded Pharisee called Saul and claimed a fugitive from justice, Moses, while he was watching sheep. So He will call you when and how He chooses— homemaker or pastor, computer programmer or refuse collector, banker or construction worker, teenager or retiree, longtime member or new Christian.

What the Lord wants is someone who loves Him and is willing to feed His sheep, who is so scared by this new opportunity that he or she must depend on the Holy Spirit and is willing to be taught. Are you ready? This will mean giving up that old, pessimistic spirit that keeps insisting, "Nothing will ever happen here." Or "The Lord can't do anything through my life. I'm too old or too young or too inexperienced or not good enough." He has always used amateurs of every age.

He might leave you right where you are, taking on a Sunday School class, visiting lonely people, opening your home to strangers, ministering to folks in prison or to those in a hospital for the mentally ill. What do you suppose it might be?

Then again, the Lord might call you elsewhere. Not to a "better situation," but to a more needy, discouraging place than the one you're in; to a short-term mission, or to live in the inner city, or to a less demanding job so you will have more time with your family.

Where does renewal start? Right now with you! Are you ready?

Chapter Two

Knowing Them by Name

*"The sheep hear His voice, and He calls His
own sheep by name and leads them out." John 10:3*

My first Sunday in the Wichita pulpit, September 7, 1975, was
not the most auspicious beginning. I was physically and emotionally rung out, having just come home five days earlier
from four intensive weeks in Southeast Asia, visiting and
participating with seven laymen in some of our pioneer mission work. On our way to a drug treatment center in an
evacuated village up the coast from Hong Kong, a couple of
our men almost drowned as we tried to ride out the heavy
swell in the South China Sea in an old weather-beaten scow.
Then we provided leadership in an exhausting but exhilarating time of renewal with almost 200 pastors from all over
South India—most of whom had walked to the conference.
Will any of us ever forget the sight and sound of most of
these men kneeling to pray as they renewed their commitment to the Lord as the conference came to a close? It was
like heavenly music. The emotional drain of walking the
streets of Calcutta, among the multitudes of wretched people
living on the streets, was relieved somewhat by our visit to
the historic William Carey Church. Then all of us shared on a
Sunday morning in different churches in Rangoon, Burma,
worshiping with faithful fellow believers so cut off from the
rest of the world.

The climax of this journey was giving leadership at a missionaries' conference at Cha-am, on the southern seashore of Thailand. Here we witnessed the Spirit working powerfully as many of these missionaries were reconciled to one another, unashamedly mingling their tears as they stood to share both their joys and frustrations. In some instances they openly asked one another for forgiveness, as when one veteran missionary spoke to another directly, "I've often disagreed with you, but it's been in the wrong spirit, and I am now asking you for forgiveness." Then the two met in an embrace of healing love.

We later learned that the Spirit evident in that service lay hold on one of the Lahu hill men who was sitting at the edge of the circle, amazed and convicted by what was taking place. This man, called "Moody" by the missionaries, went home and publicly confessed his sin of leading a double life — giving every evidence of being a holy church leader while he spent a liberal income as a secret agent for the C.I.A. in licentious pursuits. His was a costly, humiliating act which opened channels through which the Spirit could work, and revival moved from village to village borne by freshening winds of new life.

The unexpected climax of that conference was the conversion and baptism of one of the men in our party. Russ Brabec was an innovative, sensitive art professor at Sioux Falls College, and a seeker. He had joined our team at the last minute after hearing about the proposed trip at a country club luncheon. He was one of a dozen or so "spiritual mavericks" who had been drawn together to informally study the Scriptures — an uninhibited, refreshing crew. Russ was one of the people who said he would like to make the trip, but that it was out of the question.

Then less than a month before leaving I found a note on my desk scrawled on yellow legal paper: "I have decided to join you on the trip to Asia. I'm not sure what will happen, but I know I'm supposed to go. Have gone to work on the details. Russ." This kind of spontaneous response was not unusual for him. So there was a last-minute scramble for him to get everything in order. It took almost an act of Congress to get his passport and visas. Then there were the shots and arrangements for his lodging overseas, although Russ required about as little preliminary arrangement as anyone I know. Somehow it all fell into place—really the Lord's doing.

We had barely gotten into the air on the first leg of our journey, moving out over the Pacific from Los Angeles, when Russ dropped into the seat next to me and almost demanded, "Well, tell me what it's all about." I could only say, "Russ, this will not be a verbal exercise. Just listen and watch and see what happens."

At the beginning he was utterly fascinated with the Eastern art on every hand and the countless Buddhas, and snapped endless pictures from every angle.

But as we moved along we kept encountering Jesus, seeing Him through His people, like those Hong Kong druggers being healed through the love of Jesus, and their patient Pastor John. Or those faithful, childlike Indian pastors with their shining faces, so eager to serve Jesus. And then a joyful, unexpected time of renewal among the missionaries on the seacoast of Thailand. As Russ watched and listened, the Spirit drew him beyond the Buddhas and the Eastern art. In the miracle of God's grace he was brought face-to-face with the risen, conquering Lord, not in theory but in reality.

So we all wondered what Russ was up to when he stood to his feet in that last sharing session among those missionaries. The words came haltingly after a long pause, but with the warm ring of conviction, "I don't know how to say this, or where it will lead me, but I want you to know that because of what I have seen and heard here, I am declaring Jesus Christ as my Lord. I want to thank you all, particularly our team." It was a breathless moment. Russ was entering the kingdom, humble and broken. The silence was soon broken with shouts of joy, with singing and hugs. It was the music and dancing of another prodigal coming home.

That night after we had gone to bed in our outdoor dormitory, Russ quietly confessed how he had gone down to the beach that afternoon and literally buried himself in the sand, then gotten up and washed it all off. He said, "It was like I was washed clean. The old stuff had been taken from me." "Why, Russ," I said, "that's what baptism is all about. The old self is buried with Christ in His death and we rise in newness of life in His resurrected power."

"So that's what it means! Then I want to be baptized here." I could not convince him he should be baptized at home in Sioux Falls as a witness before his family and the college community. He insisted on being baptized before the people who had first heard him confess Jesus as Saviour and Lord. The next day—our last day—after sharing the bread and cup in a beautiful family Communion experience, we invited everyone to join us at the beach to celebrate the baptism of Russ Brabec. This announcement was greeted with much joy. We urged the people to remain on the shore while the visiting team—all eight of us—entered the water. But there was no way to hold anyone back. Everyone moved into the "baptismal waters" like a conquering army. It is a sight I will never forget.

Above the sound of the surf Russ spoke of being born again, and I almost shouted those words our Lord has given us, "I baptize you in the name of the Father, the Son, and the Holy Spirit." He emerged from the "watery grave" praising God with loud "hallelujahs." The Holy Spirit had truly come on him.

But there was more. On the way down to the beach, Debbie, the attractive teenage daughter of missionaries Ben and Doris Dickerson, slipped up and shyly asked, "Could I be baptized too?" Another surprise. "Yes, of course," was all I could say. "I'll call on you after Russ has been baptized." So she shared her confession of faith while the tears of many, particularly her mother and father, were mingled with the mighty waters of the Pacific. Then her father baptized her.

We reluctantly left the water and tried to partake of our last meal together, although it hardly seemed necessary, for we had eaten of that meat which is the doing of the will of the Father. We now turned toward home, where people were to hear with thanks and amazement the spontaneous confession of Russ. I later learned that he had become an unashamed evangelist on the campus of Sioux Falls College where he taught.

So I came to that first Sunday in Wichita physically and emotionally drained, ill-prepared for this new adventure, struggling to shift gears spiritually. After Ed Friesen, the chairman of the committee, had presented me to our new church family with many kind words, I could only step to the pulpit and respond, "Well, this is what you got." So much seemed to be expected from someone so needy. I was thankful for the warm laughter which greeted me.

There had been an attempt to have every able-bodied member on hand for that first service, but I was more aware of all those empty red seats in that huge sanctuary. And I wondered, as I faced these dear people, if there were many present who had not reached retirement age. I tried to preach on Paul's strong words of greeting to the Corinthian Christians, "Grace to you and peace from God our Father and the Lord Jesus Christ" (1 Corinthians 1:3). I could not help thinking that back in Sioux Falls the sanctuary would be crowded for both morning worship services with a great host of students back from the summer vacation.

Somehow I struggled through the service, climaxed by the Lord's Supper, and joined Ruth at the door to greet the people as enthusiastically as I could. Then I climbed the stairs, entered that spacious pastor's office, which seemed so strange and cold, wept a tear or two, and hurried to the private bathroom and had dry heaves. It was a lonely time. That cry of the psalmist, "How shall we sing the Lord's song in a strange land?" (Psalm 137:4, KJV) seemed to fit my situation. After I calmed down a bit, Ruth and I joined Charles and Helen McAfee, who very thoughtfully had invited us to join them for our first Sunday dinner in this new land. Their kindness was a gift.

Although there would come other times of discouragement and nostalgia, that may have been my lowest point in this new place. When I would stand at the church window staring out at the alley running between the church and the business next door and visualize the clean-cut Georgian colonial church building we had left, with its beautiful steeple and surrounded by the green lawn, I would think of all those dear friends in Sioux Falls. Some of this was self-pity, some of it uncertainty and doubt. Had we really done the right thing in moving? Could I really make this situation go? There was also the pain of adjustment. Where could I find the handles to get this new ministry underway? But at the bottom it was the evil one trying to strangle and neutralize me.

But I could not stay in that dark valley, robbed of spiritual power and creativity. The brave cadre of people we had come to serve, who had lived through so much discouragement and defeat, surrounded us with love. Their support was really the Lord's word to us in so many ways.

The warm reception and "country store food pounding" they gave us that first Sunday evening was their way of saying, "We're glad you've come." And the carefully planned installation service two weeks later, involving Baptist and community leaders, was a beautiful affirmation of our ministry.

One of the early signs of hope was a series of "get-ac-quainted coffees" in people's homes. Twenty-three of them during those first months. Ruth and I and our son, Joel, who had joined us for that year as an intern, drank enough coffee to float a battleship and ate enough pastries to start a bakery.

Betty Jane Sanderson, a dear friend since seminary days and an active member of First Baptist, had meticulously worked out all the logistics. Each Tuesday and Thursday night we were in a different home, meeting with some of our church family. Every member was invited to a nearby home, and if they were not free that night, an invitation came from another family. Apparently folks were interested in discover-ing who we really were and what we were up to, because most of the members got to one of those coffees. These gatherings opened all kinds of doors.

Night after night, after some casual visiting over coffee, I would ask them if they were willing to have a little fun getting acquainted. Of course they agreed to give it a try. What else could they say to their new pastor? I would then usually start it off by letting them know that when I was seven years of age we had lived about 100 miles north of Winnipeg, Canada, where my father was serving the Hilltop Baptist Church. I had memories from those days of wolves howling and cold winters, and of speaking Swedish in my home until I was five years of age. Then I would ask the person seated next to me where he or she had lived at age seven. So it went around the circle. There were many surprises, even among these people who thought they knew one another. How interesting to hear Glenn Marts, a man in his eighties, tell of being born on the Cherokee Strip in Oklahoma and living there until his parents moved to Wichita. Or a well-groomed woman tell of having grown up on the prairies of Nebraska and using "outdoor plumbing."

Next we asked how each of them remembered heating their homes when they were seven. For these people it wasn't gas or coal furnaces, but cow chips or corncobs or wood that had to be chopped. There would be stories of heated bricks in cold beds or huddling around potbellied stoves trying to warm up on subzero mornings. And there was much friendly laughter as these memories were shared.

We came nearer the tender center of each person's life when we asked, "Who was the person you felt closest to when you were seven?" Quite often it was a father or mother or grandparent. And frequently a schoolteacher or a friend down the block. For one person it was a dog. And none of us will ever forget the well-dressed businessman who paused and then answered with some pain, "There wasn't anyone. My mother and father were going through their second divorce when I was seven."

Finally, and here we made it clear that folks should feel

free to pass, we asked, "When did God first become real to you?" It was then we often heard beautiful, simple statements of an awakening and response to God's personal presence, particularly during the years of adolescence. And some were honest enough to confess times of doubt and struggle which finally had brought them to the certainty of God's reality. It was obvious some people were sharing their personal faith for the first time. Others, however, would say, "I was baptized when I was twelve, or fifteen, or after an evangelist had held a revival in our church." I would try to nudge them as gently as possible. "But was that when God became real to you?" That sometimes changed the response. Perhaps the most moving answer came from the one who had earlier spoken of his parents going through their second divorce. He said almost wistfully, "I don't believe God has ever been real to me."

And there were those unprogrammed happenings after the meeting, like Fritz Snodgrass showing us his woodpile and his garden. He was the highly respected retired track coach who had spent his life teaching young men to run and jump at East High and later at Wichita State University, and he could spin yarns about his boys by the hour. Fritz was eventually inducted into the Kansas Teachers Hall of Fame.

Some eight years later, the day before I conducted his funeral service, the president of Brown University called to say how sorry he was he couldn't come out for Fritz's service, but "My brother, who's an attorney in Hutchinson, will be a casketbearer. I can't tell you how much I owe Fritz—all that he taught me. He really was the dad I never had. Please give his wife my warmest greetings." And what a remarkable tribute his service turned out to be, with 100 or more of his former track men on hand, one of them coming from New Orleans. He told me at the grave how Fritz had "talked turkey" to him about his drinking problem. That challenging confrontation had been the beginning of a new life of sobriety.

Or there was the night we met Faye Perry, another retired schoolteacher, a crusty but tender woman who had taught small children for more than forty years. The "schoolmarm" spirit was still a part of her. She was the only one who showed up at the Criddlebaughs. A deep believer, she was obviously eager for this kind of fellowship. What fascinating stories she told about her family and her teaching days. And how simply and trustingly she joined us in our closing time of prayer. As we took her home she insisted Ruth and I plan to have a meal with her. So we joined her some months later in her small apartment for a delicious dinner, served in grand style. All this prepared me to stand by her as a friend later when she passed through the dark, painful valley of cancer, and finally quietly went "home."

These were rich times when we caught the ebb and flow of life among the people of First Baptist. We understood better from whence they had come, heard a bit of their hopes and dreams, and felt some of their fears and needs. I was beginning to see the "face of my parish," as Tom Allen put it long ago.

But I also had a deep conviction that a pastor should get into the homes of the people he is serving, not to check up on them—"When was the last time you read the Bible?"—or to try to persuade them to buy into some new church program, but to simply come to know them "on their turf." This is almost a quaint, outmoded notion. But how else can the shepherd come to know the sheep by name?

I know now how deeply indebted I am to my father for this conviction. He was a loving, highly respected country pastor all his active life, and more a model and a teacher than I realized, until I too became a pastor. I can well remember, as a boy hard at play, how I hated to hear my parents interrupt me, "Come in and clean up. We're going calling." I knew I was in for a long, dull afternoon unless there would be someone at one of the homes willing to play "my" kind of game. At least there would be Swedish coffee and rolls at one or more of these homes, and that meant Kool-Aid for me.

I know now that my father became a trusted friend of the people because he sought them out in their homes or in their barns, or even out in their fields. He could talk with them about the price of hogs and how the corn was doing, and often about the Saviour. During the harvest season, he usually pitched in and helped someone who was shorthanded. So his preaching and ministry was informed by and rooted in the life of his people. He knew them by name.

Richard Baxter called this "the care of souls," which can never take place in a vacuum, but always in the real situation where people are. We do not have a docetic gospel, but one of flesh and blood. Is not Jesus, who came into our world as the Incarnate Word, the great example for this style of ministry?

Think of all the obstacles and excuses and even programs that keep us from knowing our people. Can we really expect to know their names if our only contact with them is in our office at a fixed time? This can be an intimidating experience for many. And having their names organized properly in a computer does not mean we know who they are. This seems to some as detached and impersonal as a credit card operation.

All of us who are called to be shepherds can become "hirelings," professionals, for whom the cause or the ministry is more important than the people. This can happen so gradually and imperceptibly we hardly know it is taking place. And we so easily become "public figures," not only in the pulpit but in committee and board meetings, and at every community function we attend. Those biting words of Jesus, "They love to stand and pray in the synagogues and at the street corners, that they may be seen by men" (Matthew 6:5) can be true of us.

And as time goes by we get more involved, rushing from one project to another, as if none of it could happen without our being on hand. So our people say to one another, "Oh, he's so busy he wouldn't have time for me." And we can keep people at arm's length, giving an officious answer to some question they have about church life or last week's Sunday School lesson. After all, aren't we supposed to be the "answer givers"? But in doing this, we miss hearing what they really came to see us about—some great aching need at the center of their life.

And how easily we slip into office routine, shuffling papers, answering the mail, getting organized again, even playing with the computer. All that becomes so important we find it almost impossible to leave our office and go out among the people. A phone call or a knock on the door then can even become an interruption.

It is easy to begin spending so much time with a cozy "in" group, with whom we feel comfortable, that we avoid the less attractive, even cantankerous, ones. They make us feel so ill at ease. We forget that these people are often on the edge of things, longing to get "in." We can even get so lost in books and sermon preparation that we insulate ourselves from the very people for whom the sermons are being prepared.

Laziness can also be our undoing. Who else in public life has control over the schedule as we do, coming and going at our own pace and inclination? If this means sleeping in, long coffee breaks, or doodling with the office equipment, the people become like sheep without a shepherd.

Since by nature I am both a dreamer and an activist, I have constantly struggled with all of this, sometimes taking people for granted, at other times running roughshod over them trying to get the next program off the ground. And there have been days when in my need to succeed I have been more a hireling than a shepherd. It may not have seemed that way to those watching on the outside, but then they do not know my inner weaknesses as I do.

Having said all this, however, I do not want to confuse our priorities. The needs of people cannot become our god. The end of all our ministry is the glory of God, loving Him and obeying Him. To praise and worship the only true and living God is our chief calling and delight. He is the One who bids us feed His sheep—they are His and not ours. But this we cannot do unless we know and love them, which is also His gift.

So in those early days in Wichita I set out to meet our

people in their homes, usually by appointment. Most of the time I went eagerly, but sometimes reluctantly when it seemed there were more appealing things to do. Often people would ask LeeDel, my secretary, "Why is he coming? Is there something he wants me to do?" Or even, "Have I done something wrong?" But it seemed most were relieved and even grateful to discover that this would be a "getting to know you" call. A longtime secretary at the church expressed surprise when I asked for the names and addresses of the shut-ins and older members. But I felt this was where I needed to start.

What a learning experience this turned out to be, entering those places where our people lived, sitting with them, often drinking coffee, hearing a bit of their story. Some were making the best of it in a retirement home; others were alone in the great old family house; a few found themselves squeezed into some tiny apartment or even a single room; a fair number lived in spacious suburban homes; and a few were even out in farm homes. I came on a dear man, almost totally deaf, living in little more than a garage on an alley within a mile of the church. Newspapers were stacked to the ceiling around the four walls. He found some kind of security in almost compulsively picking up newspapers wherever he found them.

Our families were scattered all over—all the way from within the shadow of the church to a farm twenty miles north and everything in between. I spent more time trying to figure out the address numbering in apartment complexes than I care to admit. And this calling was not a short-term undertaking, for it stretched into months and even years.

As I came to these homes, some people seemed a bit nervous—what were they supposed to do with a pastor in the house? Most were delighted. Others, I felt, hoped this wouldn't last too long. And there were some who at first had indicated they would rather not have a pastor come by but who later learned from their friends it wasn't all that bad, and then would ask shyly, "When are you coming to see me?" At every home the welcome was genuine. "Come on in. I hear you're quite a coffee drinker. I've got some ready and I hope it's all right."

As I entered these homes I could not help noticing family pictures often prominently displayed, or some antique piece of furniture, or the plants, or the reading material scattered about. And every now and then a pet dog would give me a wet, friendly greeting, or the family cat would look with some jealousy upon my visit as an intrusion. All this said so much about the people who lived there.

But it was the conversation that mattered. Out of it all I began to hear the story of our people—so rich and varied—the memories of achievement and pain—how long it had been since Charley died or John got his medical degree. They shared the meaning of close friendships, many of them in the church, and the joys of wedding anniversaries and the birth of children and grandchildren. I wonder if anyone has seen more pictures of grandchildren than I. There were the struggles and accomplishments of work, whether in City Hall or on a used car lot, in the trust department of First National Bank or on the assembly line at Beechcraft, in the *Eagle-Beacon* advertising department or on the garbage truck route. I heard it all! And now and then there was the simple spontaneous confession of the sustaining grace of God.

How well I recall listening to a lonely widow in her large house tearfully share over coffee that I was the first pastor who had been in her home in twenty-one years. That other visit was well-remembered because it had come at the time of a tragic death in her family. And I shall always treasure calling on a beloved retired physician and his wife, Henry and Helen Loewen, whose roots were in the Mennonite tradition. They shared the intriguing story of their pioneering forebears coming to Kansas from Russia more than 100 years before, bringing with them the precious red winter wheat in trunks—which later became the backbone of the Kansas economy.

And in another home the husband and wife were obviously

the grandparents of the small, beautiful girl running about. Yet they treated her as their daughter. With great pain and hesitancy they spoke of their son serving time in one of the southern penitentiaries. The mother had left the newborn infant in a dime store in a southern city with a note pinned to the tiny bundle saying how the grandparents could be reached. Can you imagine both their hesitancy and excitement as they made the journey to bring this helpless infant home? I could understand then why these dear people watched every move of the little girl, almost as if they were afraid something might happen to her.

Usually, the visits would conclude with some moments of prayer, not as a habit, but as a continuation of our conversation, a time of blessing and thanks and intercession.

Now and then I would run into unfinished business, when I came to a home where the people had been intimately involved in the church split which had torn First Baptist asunder. Some of the disappointment and anger which had been bottled up so long might spill out! All I could do then was to hear them out. Details could become quite specific—the misunderstandings, the gossip, and the angry accusations which finally ruptured the church. Here I became to them a priest as I asked them to give all the frustration and bitterness of that experience to the only One who can finally heal our hurts. Otherwise First Baptist—this remnant we had come to serve—could never worship and serve as the people of God. This could be a day in which God would "do a new thing." Often in moments of prayer for cleansing and joy, the unmistakable power of the Holy Spirit and His gift of peace would come.

As these people entered the sanctuary Sunday by Sunday, I began to sense a new reality in our corporate worship. They were no longer strangers, but friends, fellow members. I was coming to know them by name, where they lived and who they were. And I believe they were aware that the Spirit was filling me with a love for them. There was a growing trust among us as we gathered, a rapport in the Spirit between the pastor and the congregation. But more important, a rapport between the Lord and His people, which brought new depth and power to our worship. I became less and less conscious of those empty red seats and more aware of the reality of God's presence.

More people seemed to be participating—singing the hymns with enthusiasm. What a joy when those with little musical ability would throw back their heads, open their mouths, and lift their voices in praise. People began to respond eagerly when we gave them opportunity to speak a word of praise or thanks or to voice a concern as we entered into prayer together. At times I was almost overwhelmed by the intense expectancy with which people listened to the Word of God as it was preached.

So I asked myself what should be the central theme of my preaching in these early days? How could I best help both these people and myself as we opened the Word of God together in worship? I found myself irresistibly drawn to the Epistle to the Ephesians. What better place to start than with this magnificent treatise on the wonder and calling of the church which, in spite of all its criticism and misgivings, is nothing less than the "body and bride" of Christ. The Ephesian epistle is truly a majestic hymn of praise, its lyrical phrases tumbling out, as if the writer is so gripped by the wonder of God's grace he can hardly bring any sentence to a conclusion.

The longer I studied it, worked over it, listened to it, entered into its prayers, the more I was caught up in its music. I found myself overflowing with praise and prayer to the Father, Son, and Holy Spirit. Surely this is the most "trinitarian" of all the apostles' writings. I rejoiced in the mystery of God's choosing us in Christ, discovering again I had no grounds for boasting, for I had been saved by grace, not by any work of my own, and this included anything I might think I would do in the church.

I found myself overwhelmed that I had been welcomed with all the other believers into God's "new humanity." What a company! Not held together by human resourcefulness or correct theology, or even some redemptive cause, but created by Christ, who by His shed blood has torn down every dividing wall, so that all of us who have been far off are now "no longer strangers," but "fellow citizens with the saints." That means Paul, the writer of this epistle, and John Wesley, Clarence Jordan and my beloved father, Martin Luther King and my alcoholic friend Joe McAuley are all members of the household of God which is His dwelling place in the Spirit! And what a calling has come to those of us in His body. Christ's vocation has become ours! We are to reflect His life in the world—in love, meekness, holiness, joy, forgiveness, patience—as lights shining in the darkness. Not given to drunkenness, but filled with His Spirit.

And Christ has shared gifts with us that we might be equipped for His ministry. As King David brought home "spoils" after defeating his enemies in battle and shared them with the people, so Christ has descended and done battle with all the powers of evil at the Cross, and in His resurrection has triumphed gloriously. Now He shares the spoils of that victory with His people. These are His gifts for ministry—apostleship, prophecy, evangelism, teaching and pastoring—that His body might be built up into maturity for ministry in the world. It is in yielding to His Lordship finally that we submit to one another. The family then becomes a place of unity and love, and order is brought into the structures of society. In the end all things in heaven and earth and under the earth will be united in Christ, who is the Head of the church.

I was utterly overwhelmed and renewed in this study, but how could I teach it so that all of us would understand, take it to heart, and live it out? So that these people might discover again the wonder of being the church, Christ's body?

Those dear, courageous women in the Messenger Philathea Class—most of them in their late seventies or eighties—who had heard the Bible preached ever since childhood, seated in a group toward the back on the north side; and that wiggly, eager group of young people who sat right up near the front in the second and third rows—bless them—chatting about dates and school affairs; and those wanderers and seekers who often came a bit late and sat at the very back under the balcony; and all those others in between—an intriguing mix of people. What would happen if they—and I—would hear and understand and obey the words—"Praise and Grace," "Election and Salvation," "Citizens and Members," "Calling and Gifts," "Submission and Order"? Why, it would revolutionize the church! Week after week I wrestled with that as I faced these people from the pulpit, Bible in hand.

And there were signs of hope. One of our longtime, honored members, Billymae Marts, took my arm after one service and spoke a warm, affirming word, "There's a new love coming among us." And the Rogg family made the decision to "cast their lot" with our congregation—all five of them, Ron and Deanna and their three sons—which for them would mean driving in about twelve miles from a neighboring town. Later, Ron, who became a district judge, and I would meet frequently to share and pray. Not long afterward Charlie and Carolyn Schultz and their four children came to join First Baptist, only after voicing honest misgivings about the institutional church. The baptisms of these families were glorious celebrations. And they began to bring new creative strength into our fellowship.

Then one Sunday Ed Friesen reported rather excitedly, "I saw someone here today I haven't seen for a long time—Paul and Ruby White." He went on to explain that Paul White was a longtime, well-known attorney, now partially retired—a senior partner in a large downtown law firm. The next Sunday Paul and Ruby were there again. This time they made themselves known and we had a brief visit. Some weeks later Paul invited me to join him for lunch at the Petroleum Club, his regular noontime dining place.

It turned out to be a fascinating hour and a half. Paul seemed eager to talk, as if he had been waiting for this opportunity. He spoke of his struggle to get through college, coming from very modest circumstances; his discovery that he had a love for music and what singing in the Friends University Glee Club had meant to him; how he had met Ruby and fallen in love with her and persuaded her to marry him, and of their rich, deep life together. Then he told of his decision to enter law school, and the fulfillment that had come in his practice of law, his gratitude for lifelong friendships, the richest gift of all. I was surprised and warmed by this conversation, so open and intimate.

But there was more to come. As we ended our time together he leaned forward, hesitated a moment, then spoke almost as a child, "I want you to be my friend. I walked out during all that fighting at the church, and I've missed fourteen years of life over there. Now Ruby and I are coming back." It was a sacred moment. Those phrases, "no longer strangers," "fellow citizens," "members of the household of God," were being experienced right here at the table. Christ had surely been with us in the breaking of bread.

There was only one way to respond. "Paul, I already am your friend. Perhaps I have been much longer than either of us realizes, for we are brothers in Christ." As we joined hands across the table all I could do was simply thank the Lord. Paul had come home. Some years later I was to have the privilege of leading the celebration of worship in the sanctuary for his final homegoing to the Father's house. And I shall always be grateful I had come to know his name.

Will You Come To Know the Others?

Can my church become a loving, caring, vulnerable family? A living community of compassion and healing? Well, not if we keep playing the same old game of maintenance where budgets, constitutions, building upkeep, and programs are ends in themselves, more important than people.

This is why most of us need a radical change of heart, a new way of thinking about what the church is. Let us start at the right place. This is Christ's church, not ours; His body, not an organization we have put together. He has called us to be His and chosen to dwell among us. Here we are members one of another, bearing one another's burdens, laughing and weeping with one another, forgiving one another as we have been forgiven.

So the church is deeply personal, a community of intimate, eternal relationships. We do not discover that meaning because I am casually friendly or we plan fellowship events. No, we enter into this "life together" with fellow members only when we submit to them — with all their warts and shortcomings — out of reverence for Christ. And we will spend a lifetime — even eternity — learning what that means.

Therefore, we need to be very serious about what we find out about the church in the New Testament — whose it is, who makes up its membership, what its style of life is, and what its mission is. Then we need to learn from it, explore its richness, and apply it, and let the Spirit bring us more deeply into the life of that kind of community. This needs to be experienced, not merely verbalized.

We can constantly seek out others with whom we can experience this "body life." This may start very simply, moving toward a person now and then in love, not learning only their names but who they are, and in time discovering their hopes and needs, affirming them and loving them and praying with them, sharing coffee and meals together.

We can draw together a small prayer and sharing group for support and encouragement, where people come to know one another in depth. Such an intimate fellowship can be an island of life having a contagious influence on the whole body of believers.

And is it too much to expect that in time Sunday School classes and board and committee meetings could become places of life and healing and expectancy? In the end the whole church might be renewed.

Will you be a part of this? Why not pray about it and start now?

Chapter Three

A Door Has Opened

*"Behold, I have set before you an open door,
which no one is able to shut." Revelation 3:8*

It was Monday morning and I was eager to get things done.
But here I was standing in the church hallway fumbling with
a hidden latch, trying to open a swinging Dutch door so I
could get my mail. I was still new, not yet knowing all the
idiosyncrasies of the system. Carol Morgan, the friendly
young woman at the reception desk, apparently sensed my
frustration because she expressed my feelings as she greeted
me. "We just keep too many things locked up around here,
don't we?"

But if a congregation has been torn up by misunderstanding and bitterness climaxed by a drawn-out struggle in the
courts, and finally the state Supreme Court rules that "your"
group is entitled to the building, how do you avoid "locking
up"?

The building can now be a kind of "security blanket" which
must be watched over zealously. The pianos and the kitchen
and the boiler and the Communion equipment and everything
else must be carefully guarded. Meeting the mortgage pay-
ments regularly becomes a major accomplishment. All this
seems to say to outsiders, "This building is sacred territory
which belongs to us. Watch your step!"

And the church constitution—painstakingly written line by

line—now reflects this "locking up" attitude. Rather than being a liberating guide for congregational life and ministry, it becomes a defensive document, saying by implication, "No one is going to steal the horse out of the barn this time."

Now the major topic of a business meeting can become the "money item," the fear that there will not be enough to meet the expenses. Questions like, "Where can we cut back?" or "Can we get the leaky pipes fixed?" or "Aren't we paying the staff too much?" can dominate the meeting. The central issues of church life are now bypassed or hurried over because there is no time left to deal with these deeper matters so that the church has a sense of mission and direction:

- What is the Lord's will for this church now?
- Are we becoming more and more a praying, maturing people?"
- What is our strategy to reach and win lost people for Christ?
- How can we support and strengthen family life, including the single-parent home?
- How can this great building be used more frequently as a place of outreach?
- Are there ministries of mercy and righteousness to which Christ is calling us in this community?

It seems that some people come to business meetings expecting to "protect the constitution." For them, Robert's Rules of Order is the last word in doing the Lord's business. They expect to untangle motions sometimes hastily made, followed by amendments and substitute motions, with human rules rather than seeking for Divine wisdom. We can know this wisdom only when we turn to the New Testament and prayerfully seek for the mind of Christ and the unity of His Spirit.

Even the way people seated themselves during worship in that vast sanctuary seemed to reflect that "locked out" mentality. Some clustered in their own little group usually toward the back, as if they did not want a new person to break in. And the people seated on the north side often did not know those sitting on the south side. Even during a fellowship time, some people were quite reluctant to move toward a new person fearing they might discover this "stranger" to be a longtime member. And here and there people would be sitting alone, isolated from the other worshipers, longing to be included.

But what other way was there for this remnant to carry on? Even after Max Morgan, a strong pastor, had led the people valiantly for nine years, and Ray Parry had been their interim pastor for two and one-half years and had "helped the people laugh again," as one member put it, they were still asking, "What is the future of the congregation?" It was a time of waiting and groping for direction, a time for wondering, "Should we exchange this great building, for which we have sacrificed so much, but is so costly to maintain, for the smaller building of Central Christian two blocks away which is bulging at the seams with people?" Or, "Should we try to sell our property and move out to the suburbs?" But the people kept hanging on. This was their place and somehow they believed this was to be the base of their ministry.

Many of them could not help contrasting the glories of the past with the present situation. Now only a small congregation came to worship in the great sanctuary which once was filled Sunday morning and evening. And it was very seldom anyone came to join the church or accept Christ, although once there was hardly a service when someone did not come to publicly confess faith in Christ. While the Sunday School continued with a number of strong adult classes, there were scores of classrooms standing empty week after week. Now only one or two babies were in the nursery Sunday morning, where formerly several nurseries were filled with little ones. And where could enough money be found to meet the building debt and pay the utility bills, with anything left over for staff and program? The income from renting office space on the fourth floor of the Christian Education building to a variety of religious organizations and fellowship hall to a Quaker congregation came nowhere near paying the cost of maintenance.

But it was the sale of all kinds of Sunday School equipment, particularly from the children's department, to help keep things going, that raised the question most painfully, "Is there a future for this church?"

In the face of all this, was there any way this faithful band would risk opening its life to become again a vulnerable, healing family? So it seemed Carol's greeting that day, "There are too many things locked up around here," was far more than an expression of frustration. It may have spoken the deepest hopes and best impulses of these brave, stubborn people—a holy dissatisfaction with things as they were and a longing for something better.

And in those early months we were to discover, literally stumble into, unexpected situations and opportunities where the doors began to open a bit. Not accidental happenings, we later learned, but part of "a divine strategy."

One of these surprises involved our youngest son, Joel. At the time of his graduation from Ottawa University, he had quietly suggested that perhaps he could come to Wichita to "help out" for a year. I was a bit taken aback by his offer. This was all so strange and new coming from Joel, the most reticent and inward of our three children. Only recently had he entered into the life of the Spirit.

He had struggled to find himself—floundered in his first years of college trying to be a "jock," one of the boys, and had finally dropped out to come home to take on any work he could find. The first job was in a bowling alley, then a summer with a highway improvement crew, then working for a stretch at Du-Al Manufacturing, and finally a summer in mobile home construction with a dear friend, Don Ebert, in Bismarck, North Dakota. The two of them seemed to need each other, struck up a great friendship, and played countless games of Ping-Pong. After that summer I could hardly ever beat Joel at Ping-Pong.

But all during this time Ruth and I were aware of a restless confusion, a drift, in our son's life. He seemed "bottled up." We could only wait and hope that one day he could let it out.

The climax came when I was called to the phone during a dinner with some friends. Ironically we were meeting with Nicky Cruz to discuss the problem of drug abuse which was just beginning to surface in the schools in our community. The voice on the phone asked if I was the father of Joel Fredrikson. When I responded affirmatively, somehow aware this was not an ordinary phone call, he identified himself as a police officer in Vermillion, South Dakota, the university town. Then he reported they were holding Joel in jail. They had found him acting strangely on one of the streets and brought him in high on drugs. I managed to say I'd be right down, although my heart was beating like a trip-hammer and my mouth seemed full of cotton. I died a dozen deaths during that seventy-mile drive to Vermillion, asking myself repeatedly, "Where did we go wrong? How did we fail Joel? What will he be like?"

The police mercifully insisted there would be no charges. As one of them said, "In this college town we have to deal with this kind of thing all the time." They reported that someone named Jim, who came around the jail once in awhile, whom I have never met but to whom we will be eternally grateful, had "talked Joel down out of his 'high.'" When I saw our son I could only greet him with gratitude and relief.

Years later Joel sent me a Peanuts Father's Day card with Snoopy pictured on the cover saying, "Without you I feel like an abandoned orphan." Then he had scrawled, "I remember the evening thousands of years ago in a jailhouse in Vermillion, South Dakota. The moment you walked in, the love of Christ was on your face and the question you asked first was, 'Are you okay?' That has and always will stick with me. At my darkest hour your love came through." What an affirmation. Surely my greeting him that way was a gift of God's grace. For I remember neither the words I spoke nor how I said them.

It was a quiet, painful drive home, with only a sentence spoken now and then. "Now, Dad, don't you and Mom blame yourselves. You've been great parents." How thankful I was to hear that. When I could not keep from asking him, "Why did you get into this?" he answered, "Because I wanted to get out of the boundaries of my mind." Then I drew a deep breath and asked, "How long?" He said, "A year and a half and I've tried most everything." I could only assure him that Ruth and I loved him, and that nothing could change that. We were open to him and would do anything we could to help him. I hoped there was no false pressure in my saying, "Joel, your mom and I turned you over to the Lord a long time ago, and whatever happens, you're in His keeping." This does not come easily for me. I am too prone to manage, to hang on. When we got home, Joel and his mother had a tearful, beautiful reunion.

The next semester Joel went back to college. We could only hope and pray. When he came home for the spring break he dropped the good news on us, quietly and unexpectedly, at our first meal together. When a lull finally came in the conversation, he said, "I have something I must tell you. I have been baptized in the Holy Spirit." He said it so off-handedly, but with such feeling, it took our breath away. It was then I noticed the warm glow on his face. We could only weep with joy. "How did it happen?" We were eager to know, aware that our Lord always deals with us so graciously and unexpectedly.

Stanley DeFries, the head of the music department at Ottawa and a longtime friend, had seen Joel passing by, thrown open a window in old Tauy Jones Hall, and called, "Hey, Joel, why don't you try out for 'Most Happy Fella,' a musical comedy we're going to be doing later in the spring?" He brushed it off. "Thanks, I'll think about it," as he hurried off to class. Why, he wouldn't have a chance of landing a part. He wasn't in choir or even taking voice lessons. But the invitation came again the next day through the same open window. And later again. Finally, somewhat reluctantly, Joel did try out. He didn't know if he could handle another defeat. What a shock when he was given a part—not just any character, but Joey, one of the leads. We later discovered that Stanley's wife, Alice Jo, was the real heroine of this whole episode. She had believed through thick and thin there was something beautiful, almost hidden, in Joel's life that would surprise everyone if it could only be called forth.

And Joel began to discover there was music in him. He was gifted. As people listened and thanked him, a new confidence came. He no longer had to force himself to make it in sports. Now all kinds of music began to pour forth, some of it sung out of his own experience, and more and more of it to the praise of God.

At the same time a sensitive, caring college chaplain, Fred Gibson, invited Joel to come in for a visit, knowing nothing of Stanley's invitation. Another serendipity! Fred was gentle, but very direct, and the timing was perfect. "God's trains always run on time." He made it abundantly clear that he loved Joel or he would not be taking this risk. Ever since he had known him he had sensed something lacking, a need, in Joel's life. Did he want to do anything about it? The power of Christ could cleanse and renew him. Suppose they prayed together? And as Joel shared this with us he said, "I wanted to, but I held back because I didn't know if I was going to climb the walls or dance on the backs of the chapel pews, or what was going to happen. But finally I said, 'Yes, let's go ahead.' When we knelt and started to pray, half of me began to cry and the other half was laughing. I guess that went on for almost half an hour." A time of infilling, of drinking living water, of joy and release. "The old has passed away, behold, the new has come."

Little wonder then that after Joel had shared his heart with us we went out into the night and walked under the starlit skies, rejoicing and praising the One who makes all things new.

Now here it was a year later at graduation time, and Joel was saying, "I think maybe I ought to spend a year with you in Wichita helping out any way I can." He knew this was what he was called to do, even though I held back. I have always been leery of "father-son acts" in the ministry. But during that summer, while Joel was serving on an Ottawa Gospel team, an interview was arranged with the church personnel committee. Terry Walter, the chairman, had more vision and courage than I, or some members of the congregation who wondered what this bearded, untried novice had to offer. I was surprised a few days later when Terry called to announce, "Well, we've decided to call Joel as an intern for a year. We've asked him to lead our choir and strengthen our youth program."

So that fall we began our ministry together in this great old downtown church, so much of it new and different. But none of it was more challenging than our relationship, not only as father and son, but now as colleagues in ministry. When either of us said, "Let's have a staff meeting," it usually meant my taking Joel to lunch. The salary of an intern doesn't allow for too much entertaining. A bit different than Sioux Falls where we had four ordained pastors and a business manager on our staff.

Joel and I learned from each other. How well I remember letting my frustration spill out after a Sunday morning service, "When in the world are we going to have 300 people in that sanctuary?" Joel put it to me straight, "Dad, the Lord has to teach you a few lessons before that can happen." That, coming from the mouth of this "inexperienced" son. But it was a word that has come home to me again and again.

Then there was the afternoon Joel said he had to see me. I saw the look of fear in his eyes as he came into the office and closed the door. And tears came as he blurted out his feelings, not easy for him. "I'm really scared. This is bigger than I realized and I don't think I'm up to it." I could only share some of my own fears with him—how I am often a scared, little boy even though I might seem to exude confidence, and the times I have had to confess, "I've tried to do it in my own strength again, Lord. Forgive me and teach me once more to trust You." Then Joel and I knelt in prayer. It was a tender, renewing moment.

After he had gone I thought, "I must share something of myself with Joel as a pledge of support." Then I noticed the simple cross made of burnt matches on the wall, a gift I had received from Al Sapp, an alcoholic friend, some years earlier. This was it! Again there were tears when I told him this was a part of my life, a gift from another who had shared out of his gratitude. It became a sign between us that the Lord's power can be revealed only through our weakness. I have noticed ever since that wherever Joel has been, that cross has been hanging in a special place.

At Joel's first choir practice no one was more nervous than his mother, who has sung in church choirs all her adult life, under some very outstanding directors. "I don't know what I'll do if anyone criticizes him," she said. "I know I'll really get defensive." But he took hold with enthusiasm and was utterly honest with the people who gathered. "I've never directed a church choir before, and I know I'm going to make some mistakes, and so will you. But if we work at it together, I know we can share some beautiful music to the glory of God."

This eager beginner was not held back by the fear of being compared to other musicians, but plunged ahead, encouraging the choir to sing some of the music he had learned in the college concert choir. It was strong stuff for some of the less experienced people, but they were challenged and gave their best. Joel was warmed by the encouragement of many of the veteran choir members. I can still see these dear people processing up the aisle, holding their hymn books high, singing as if their lives depended on it. By Christmas they were singing Bach's "For Unto Us a Child Is Born."

Then one afternoon I was called by the chairman of the music committee. "We really think it would be better if Joel didn't come to the music committee meeting tonight." When I asked, "Why?" the answer was, "Some of the people are a bit concerned about the kind of clothes Joel is wearing in worship. They feel he is really dressed too casually to be leading in worship." I had never told Joel what to wear. After all, he was twenty-two years of age, and it was a miracle he was even in a church trying to direct a choir.

I sensed here the "closed door" attitude—institutional restriction in conflict with an accepting family spirit. Must people always wear the right clothes, use a particular language, act a certain way, to fit the expectations of the organized church? Or can it be a place, a sanctuary, a gathering where sinners and seekers wearing jeans and sneakers, or black suits and ties, could feel welcome, at home? Coming to know together the grace and forgiveness of the living God?

All this went through my mind, but my answer was simply, "We're trying to be an open church, so if we are going to discuss the clothes a person wears, or anything else, that person should be present. Otherwise we end up with 'we's' and 'they's' and the body of Christ becomes divided. And Joel is a big boy. He can take care of himself."

Joel's report later that night was both humorous and hopeful. Yes, the "clothes issue" had come up at the end of the meeting. After the regular agenda had been completed, one of the members cleared his throat a couple of times before bringing it up. "Joel, there's something personal we need to discuss with you. It has to do with the kind of clothes you wear when you direct the choir Sunday mornings." Joel could only ask, "Is there a problem?" "People are complaining, saying your clothes really are too casual for a Sunday morning service." "Well," Joel asked, "who are these people?" "We'd rather not say." To which Joel responded, "Some of the young people think it's great that I dress in my own way. I guess it's a question of who we are ministering to, isn't it?" Then, "Besides, I have only one suit in addition to my jeans and sports clothes."

So the discussion went on for a bit. "What is proper? To whom are we ministering? How much freedom can we allow our intern to have?" In the end the committee gave Joel a beautiful affirmation. "You wear what you feel right and comfortable in, and we'll support you." Two weeks later Joel came into worship wearing not only a choir robe but a big grin.

This was no new, earthshaking decision, but a small positive step. One of the doors had begun to open a crack. The renewal of congregational life does not come by an official vote in a business meeting or through a major program launched from the front office, but by small, quiet acts of obedience here and there which begin to open channels through which the winds of the Spirit can blow. Such was the case, I believe, when that music committee decided to let a young man be himself.

Near the end of Joel's year with us there was the case of the "missing piano." He discovered that the Good News Circle with Bob Laurent, a team unusually gifted in evangelism with youth, was available for a few days in August. Again there was church approval, although from a human standpoint it seemed like a ridiculous undertaking. How could we get ready in such a short time, and would anyone be willing to show up for a "spiritual affair" in August? But the people took hold and began to make preparations, enlisting people to lead out in prayer and handle the counseling, publicity, finances, and all the rest.

One of those early morning meetings of preparation stands out vividly. There was an unusual spirit of anticipation as we gathered at the Holiday Inn on North Broadway. The group seemed to anticipate that God was about to do something beautiful. I could not help noticing a strong junior high boy, Steve Schultz, seated next to his father, Charlie—a great team. There was a look of intense wonder on the young man's face. His whole demeanor was saying, "I don't want to miss a thing. I'm in this all the way." This has characterized Steve's life to this day. He is now a committed high school science teacher with a keen concern for his students.

It was agreed that these "Good News" meetings should be on "neutral ground." We had a natural site one block from the church, the Orpheum Theater. We leased a grand but vacant historic landmark, even though the rent for the four nights was $1,200, and there was a great deal of work to do cleaning up the dirt and the "contributions" of the pigeons. I watched all of these arrangements unfolding under Joel's leadership with a kind of wonder.

Then on the eve of the first service, Alan Cowles, a faithful, concerned brother who was helping care for our church building, came rushing into my office breathlessly. "The baby grand in the parlor has been stolen." What! Why this was preposterous! How could a massive piano be carried off in broad daylight? Could Alan be dreaming? All this went through my mind as I hurried off with him to check things out. Sure enough, the piano was gone. Then as Alan was about to call the police a light began to dawn: "Joel — Good News Circle — Orpheum Theater — music — piano." That was it! I could only say, "Alan, hold it. We're going to the Orpheum Theater to check out this stolen piano." And there was the baby grand in all its shining glory. Joel had gotten some men and a truck and they had moved the piano.

To him it was very simple. You have a need. The church has a piano. You move it. That was opening the door too much, too fast — even for me. So I gently explained to him something of "institutional protocol," "clearing" with the proper committee for what needs to get done. Joel seemed to understand — somewhat!

Of course, there must be church approval to move a valuable piano out of the building even a block for an evangelistic affair. But bypassing the "approval process" underlines youthful impatience with the frustrating intricacies of the way church decisions are often made — endless discussions about some issue as it moves from committee to committee, while earnest, well-meaning people try to come to some decision, then often giving the responsibility for carrying it out to a person who is accountable to no one. Is it any wonder that sometimes our most gifted people simply say, "I have no interest in getting involved in that kind of game"?

And, sad to say, even when a decision has been made it can

be thwarted or blocked by those who insist that any action must be "cleared" with them, whether or not they hold any church office. There is that hidden power structure which can quietly control institutional church life. These are the ones who presume to know what is best for everyone, "and no one is going to do anything around here until we've got the money in hand." There are those whose feelings are hurt if they are not consulted. "My family has invested lots of effort and money in this church and I need to know what's going on." And often there are those with "turf" to protect. "This is *my* room, *my* Sunday School class, *my* program, or *my* piano, and no one is going to move it or change it unless I give approval."

So a congregation can feel hemmed in, and become fearful and indecisive while Christ's real work of redemption and healing never gets done. There are too many former pastors selling insurance and pumping gas—and with heavy hearts—because they did not want to spend the rest of their lives trying to deal with the institutional games of immature church people.

But we have a model pattern for handling our church affairs in one of the first major decisions made by the early church, so adolescent but so full of life and power. Among those first 3,000 converts were Greek widows being left out in the "daily distribution." Had this wrong not been dealt with in the right spirit, these early believers could have split into two camps—the "First Jewish Church of Christ" and the "Zion Avenue Gentile Christian Church." But guided by the Spirit, the Twelve called the whole body together. They made it clear in that congregational meeting they could not neglect their calling of "preaching the word," even though "serving tables" was a crucial ministry. Consequently, seven helpers were chosen, gifted for the feeding ministry, men who had a "good reputation," and who were "full of the Spirit and of wisdom. And what they said pleased the whole multitude" (Acts 6:5). And what was announced was done! Little wonder that with that spirit of harmony and obedience "the word of

God increased; and the number of the disciples multiplied greatly in Jerusalem" (Acts 6:7). Whenever we do the business of the Lord His way, not our way, we can expect to witness "great signs and wonders."

Something akin to this seemed to happen with the "Good News" event in the Orpheum. There was a need and an opportunity and the people moved with one mind to meet it. So we celebrated four glorious nights together. All kinds of people, mostly young, thronged the theater each night, filling the air with beautiful songs of praise to the glory of God—accompanied by that baby grand piano. And the Gospel was preached, simply and persuasively, with scores moving to the front each night to openly confess Christ!

Almost immediately after this celebration, Joel left for Bethel Seminary. He now knew this was the next step in his journey. He had been right all the time. God wanted him in Wichita for *that* year. Now he had finished what he had been sent to do. There was no way we could ever shut some of the doors that had been opened!

But another door of opportunity was all around us—our neighborhood. I could not help wondering day after day, as I drove down to our church building, about the people who lived near the church. Who were they? Did they even know we existed? Did we care about them? Yes, our congregation had made the decision to stay at Second and Broadway. But did our people understand that simply being there was a calling to minister to those in the shadow of the church? Not just to those who drove in from the suburbs and the surrounding communities?

One day I voiced this concern to Vic and Elaine Evans, longtime friends ever since they had been in my New Testament class at Ottawa University. They were open, hospitable people whose home was always open to the stranger. Their response was immediate and warmly positive. Vic and Elaine had been hoping for some time that we might go out among these people in our neighborhood and meet them as friends. They were eager to help if we decided to go ahead. So together we began to ask how this might be done.

Whenever the Lord lays a need on someone's heart and kindles a vision for meeting that need, He calls forth laborers for that mission, then gifts and empowers them that the harvest may be taken. When the Apostle Paul accepted that urgent "Macedonian call," the fun really started. Suppose he had hung back. Think what he would have missed! Too many churches lose out on that kind of exciting adventure because they are afraid to be spiritually stretched. They have squeezed their whole ministry into what they can handle comfortably. That's when they begin to die.

Now calling in the neighborhood of a downtown church in Wichita, Kansas may not have been a major event like the Apostles taking the Gospel into Europe. But for us it was an open door into the heart of our city. Those people in our neighborhood, whom we did not know, became the Macedonian call. We could hear them saying, "Come over and help us," and we would lose precious spiritual ground if we did not respond. Our church leaders gave their blessing, even though some voiced misgivings. Some of them probably felt, "The pastor is new and we should be willing to support some of his ideas."

Our plan was very simple. We would ask for volunteers to go out two by two within a four-block radius of the church building. Each team would call at every door wherever they found people — in rooming houses, apartment buildings, or hotels — on one side of the street for a two-block stretch. We would move out on our mission after a light lunch on a Sunday afternoon. Vic and Elaine would work out the assignments and I would share some simple instructions and words of encouragement before the people took off. We would report back after the calls.

To our delight, fifty-six people showed up for this venture, quite excited and nervous, but willing to give it a try. "I've never done anything like this before, but I'm glad I don't have to go alone." We asked that they simply go to every door on their side of the street, knock, and identify themselves as friends, and not be shocked by anything they might find.

They were to share three things. First, "We've come because we care." If they could not honestly say that, it would be better they not go, and we would bless them and thank them for having come this far. No one left! Second, "The most important word we can share with you is that God loves you, regardless of how you may feel or who you are." Third, "Is there anything we can do to help you?" Here there was risk, for that could mean personal involvement. There was to be no card signing, no embarrassing questions, no preaching. Each couple did have a few copies of *Good News for Modern Man*, which they could leave if people wanted them. So we prayed—fervently and hopefully—and left on our mission.

The field into which we went was varied and challenging. All around were the evidences of the struggle within the inner city. There were signs of renewal and hope—the gleaming steel and glass of Bank IV; the beautiful new office building for Misco, a petroleum firm; and the handsome old building that had been restored to house radio station KFH; plus the plans for exciting new downtown buildings. But there were also the signs of decay and death—the grand old homes on North Broadway, now faded rooming houses; the aging buildings that once bustled with business activities, now standing empty and forlorn; the hotel across the alley from the church, now the temporary home for former prison inmates who were in the Work Release program.

And hidden in little rooms or apartments off darkened hallways, and upstairs in buildings with no life downstairs, were all kinds of people—far more than I had realized. Young marrieds trying to get started; older folks, mostly single women, struggling to get along on a Social Security or welfare check; a growing number of Hispanics and refugees from Southeast Asia hoping to make it in this new culture; and a surprising number of alcoholics. These were the people we went out to meet that Sunday.

Ruth and I drew the north side of Douglas from Broadway to Emporia Street, and started on our journey. We were certain that after we passed the Looking Glass, a drinking and eating establishment frequented by the yuppie crowd, we would not find any people. But as we climbed the stairs of a couple of older, evacuated buildings, we found a few folks almost hidden away in small rooms. And they received us gladly, as if we were at least a diversion from the boredom of another long Sunday afternoon. I could not help wondering, "How many people in this city are sitting waiting for someone to come?"

Toward the end of our assignment we came on two of our callers, Clara Haynes and Islo Garner. An unlikely pair to be doing this sort of thing, I thought. But they were having the time of their lives. However, they didn't want to go into the Eaton Hotel, one of the stops on their assignment, without some company. The Eaton is a grand old landmark, one of the places where "Hatchet Carrie Nation" is reported to have smashed all the booze bottles within reach, in her battle with the liquor traffic. It is now a refuge for men and women coming in off the streets for a few nights, provided they are sober. So we entered the great lobby with its marble floor, identified ourselves, and spoke a few words of encouragement to the men lounging in the well-worn chairs.

Then Ruth and I crossed the street for our last stop at the Renfro Hotel, a seedy way station for transients, a couple of notches socially below the Eaton. Here we found one man slouched over in a chair, having body jerks, struggling with a hangover, obviously not interested in visiting with anyone. But the woman behind the desk was eager to tell us about herself. She had done an exceptionally poor job of tinting her hair orange-red and there was no escaping the aroma of her cheap perfume. When she discovered why we had come, she immediately told us she was a "fallen away Baptist." But she was visibly touched when we assured her she would be given a warm welcome by the people at our First Baptist "wayside station," particularly at one of our Wednesday night fellowship suppers. The only audible prayer we uttered during our visits was in the lobby of the Renfro.

Then we hurried back to the church to hear what had taken place. As we entered fellowship hall, people were sharing their reports with shouts of laughter. They were not only relieved because they had survived the calls, but delighted that they had been given a welcome beyond anything they expected. Those they visited were eager to talk when they found out it wasn't a pressure call. Ed Friesen had come on a man who had responded to his greeting, "Oh, yes, you expelled me from school when you were principal." And Clara and Islo were asked simply, "Pray for us," at one of the places they had visited.

And, of course, here and there people did not want to be bothered. Some were too fearful of any stranger to come to the door, and a few were sleeping off hangovers. But the joy of all those places where we were received far outweighed the disappointment of the closed doors.

Some did share their needs. "I can hardly see anymore. Do you suppose someone would come and read to me once in awhile?" "Could you come and help me get my groceries when my check comes? I can't walk very far and I have no car." "I'm so lonely. It would be wonderful if you would just come and talk with me now and then." The call for help had come and we could not duck our responsibility.

This is no great success story. There was no sudden influx of people from the neighborhood clamoring to join our church. We are called to faithfulness, not to the success of numbers. But we discovered we were surrounded by a mission field. And through that downtown grapevine the word went out that maybe there were some people at a church who cared.

A few relationships were established that became friendships—the beginning of a caring network. And some came eventually to cast their lot with us. Our church family would have been far poorer if Gladys Lott and John George, Anna Grissom and Edith Mott and others had not come to share their lives and gifts with us. Little did we know at the outset how much they were going to teach us.

Months after Joel had gone to seminary we came on a green card on which he had written a name, Red Avery, and an address with a comment or two. Ruth and I agreed finding that card was the Lord's way of saying, "I want you to go and see this man," which we did, bringing cookies and a thermos of coffee. We found him living downstairs in a nondescript gray house. Red had struggled for years with his drinking habits and his speech was impaired because of a stroke. At first he was suspicious, but he brightened a bit when we showed him the green card.

Something, better to say Someone, kept bringing us back to see Red, every month or so, with a snack. And difficult as the conversation was, we became friends. We learned a little about his family and his work as a mechanic. Then discovered that the owner of the liquor store next door, who was Red's landlord, had arranged to receive his disability check each month and, after taking out the rent money, would also keep some for the booze he pushed off on Red. It was a vicious circle, in which this lonely man was caught. As we were trying to discover how this injustice could be corrected, Red was moved to a home for the aging. We called on him once there before reading some weeks later in the obituary section that Red Avery had died. It was that simple. I recall now how attentive he had been whenever we read a few verses of Scripture and how reverent he was when we prayed. Red had opened a door for us. We had seen Christ in him, "the least of these."

Often adversity becomes the door of opportunity. So it was when an almost unbearable heat wave hit Wichita for most of July in 1980. Day after day during that month the temperatures climbed to 100 degrees and more—one day 115 degrees. And there was little change at night. The earth lay parched and cracked, almost panting for some relief. And each time the wearying, frazzled people saw even the hint of a cloud they wondered, "Can this be it? Will some blessed rain come our way today?"

But it was the "little people"—those neighbors of ours—

who were almost frying in their small rooms with no air conditioning. So an urgent appeal went out from the Red Cross. Were there any churches or other public buildings that would open their doors to these people suffering in the heat?

One of our dear people heard that cry and responded. Vickie Helm was a younger, spontaneous, and utterly outspoken new believer. She was so noninstitutional in her ways I was really surprised when she and Bruce decided after much struggle they would be baptized and become a part of the people of First Baptist.

Several years before, Bruce's sister Barbara had prevailed upon me to officiate at their marriage, which I agreed to do only after visiting with them and discovering how serious they were about making a go of it. Somehow I felt this was right even though both of them had made all kinds of mistakes in previous relationships and had little or no interest in the institutional church.

It was a most unusual wedding on New Year's Eve day in a social center. The minute I walked in I knew this was not the typical church crowd. The best man, I discovered, operated a bar called the "Devil's Paw." But as soon as I uttered the first words, "Dearly beloved, we are gathered here in the presence of God to join this man and this woman in holy marriage . . ." the casual, easy-going banter gave way to a solemn hush. What a tremendous opportunity! The Lord was surely in that place.

Two years later at Christmastime Bruce called. It was our first contact since the wedding. "We thought we might come to church tomorrow. How do you get into the building?" Another surprise. "You will have no problem getting in. We have all kinds of doors, and we'll be delighted to have you." And they were there! As they left after worship one of them commented, "This really wasn't too bad." How refreshingly honest. I was only too happy to oblige when they wondered if I could come by and see them.

When I came to their small, comfortable home on a cold, snowy day, they did not waste time on trivial talk but were eager to get at some of the big questions that had been haunting them, hungering as they were for spiritual reality. What a time we had—a far more interesting and meaningful conversation than one often has in so many "churchy" circles, sad to say. They brought out a *Good News for Modern Man* someone had given them, wondering "What kind of a book is this?" And they agreed to read the Gospel of Mark. My heart was singing as I left.

Bruce and Vickie were utterly serious! In time they met Jesus and heard His simple call and, like Matthew, left their old ways—including their marijuana—to follow Him! And their growth in obedience got them into all kinds of Christian predicaments—adopting a lovely, neglected child; journeying to New York to share their witness in an evangelism conference; befriending a variety of "stray sheep"; challenging the church to get into a "Mom's Day Out" ministry; and how much else the Lord only knows.

So when Vickie heard the call for help that desperately hot July, there was only one thing to do: challenge the church into opening its air-conditioned fellowship hall to some of these people.

Often new believers best understand what the followers of Jesus are expected to do. They naively believe they are to simply obey their Lord. They have not yet become tamed and domesticated by compromises and rationalizations. As Vickie wrote later, "I started off Monday morning so excited and eager to open the doors of 'our church,' God's house, to people in need of a shelter." And in spite of those who wondered if the church building should be "used for this kind of thing," and those who verbally supported her but were unwilling to sign up as volunteers, Vickie hung on and won the day.

It may have been providential that we were out of town, because now Vickie could not ask "Big Daddy," as she called the senior pastor, to help out. So she made her appeal to Jim Holt, our associate, for support! Now he had to decide—a stretching, growing experience. Particularly when the call came at night and the decision could not be delayed. Jim made the bold move. "Vickie, you go ahead and let the Red Cross know they can count on us. And I'll get the proper permission through the channels in the morning."

Now the issue had really been raised. "Do we dare let strangers in, particularly some of those people we see around us?" "We didn't realize when we decided to stay downtown we'd be called on to do this kind of thing." But in the end those people who had to affirm or veto the decision, those practical men and women on the "property and services" committee, understood what was at stake and approved what was being done. Christ had come to our door through these people, and thank God we heard His voice and opened the door. "I was a stranger, and you took Me in."

That understanding was not unanimous. Not everyone was jumping up and down with joy over having these folks in "our church basement." This was a mystery to Vickie, who later wrote, "I find it so hard to understand how come everyone doesn't want to serve our Lord by offering a cup of cold water. (I'm starting to sound like a Christian, huh?)"

What a surprise I was in for when, unaware of any of these happenings, I came home from vacation for a special business meeting. I had no sooner entered the door when someone grabbed me by the arm. "Let me show you who we have in fellowship hall," like we were entertaining someone very special. And we were. For here I came on the most unusual gathering of people I had ever seen in our church building — black and white, young and old, a couple seated in rocking chairs, some playing cards, some drinking coffee, others watching a TV which had just been brought in.

As I moved among these new friends, little was said, only a handshake or a "Glad to meet you." Yet a spirit of childlike gratitude, a sense of being at home, seemed to fill the room. Almost as if these people were saying, "This is where we belong." And that included a seventy-eight-year-old woman and Carol Whaley, whose apartment thermometer read 114 degrees, who brought her overheated small daughter,

Christa, with a fever of 103 degrees. And those words of admonition by the writer of the Letter to the Hebrews came to mind, "Do not neglect to show hospitality to strangers, for thereby some have entertained angels unawares" (Hebrews 13:2).

Suppose we would have turned aside from this opportunity, saying, "We've got too much going on already. We can't take on this added burden." We would have been a poorer congregation, less Christ's people—and missed "entertaining angels."

In a few days the worst of the heat had passed and our new friends returned to their homes. But they left knowing the doors of this place were open and we knew we could never go back to where we had been before they came. And it was Vickie, a new Christian who did not know any better than to obey, who helped us walk through an open door.

Where Are the Open Doors?

Can anything new happen in the ordinary places where we find ourselves? Everything seems so dull and routine, so locked up. Any change seems so impossible because each time we propose a new venture or a different way of doing things we hear the same old refrain, "We've never done that before," or "We don't have the money to try that."

Yet we claim to worship and serve a living God who has always shown up in unexpected places pulling off some kind of serendipity. An old man and woman laughing hilariously because the Lord has made good on His promise to give them a baby. Joshua marching around a mighty city with a motley crew blowing trumpets until the walls come tumbling down. Jesus walking out of His own grave, the risen, conquering Lord. We talk in our churches about all these happenings. But has that kind of thing ended? Has the Lord gone on vacation?

Perhaps we have become spiritually paralyzed, succumbing to a spirit of pessimism and defeat—favorite tricks of the Evil

One. Now our reaction has become, "So what?" or "It can't happen." That living expectancy we once knew is gone. So is there anything we can do? Yes, there is!

1. Read again the Acts of the Apostles, thoughtfully and prayerfully, as if you were reading this amazing story of God at work for the first time. Underline every situation where the Lord did the impossible through "ordinary people." All the way from that incredible sermon Peter preached on the Day of Pentecost to Paul's witness as a prisoner in the midst of a shipwreck on the way to Rome. Let all this be contemporary! Tell the Lord you dare to believe He can do it again right where you are!

2. Then ask the Lord to forgive you for your own timidity and lack of faith. Be specific! If you have been crippled by a spirit of doubt and pessimism, confess it and ask Him to set you free. The evil one has held you back long enough!

3. Now ask the Lord to fill you with His Spirit of optimism and hope. There are open doors all around, opportunities almost hidden, which only He can help you see—the people living within the shadow of the church who seem so disinterested; that lonely woman recently divorced, trying desperately to make it with three children, who shows up once in awhile; that Sunday School class that seems to be dying of lethargy; the stubborn, demanding boss with whom you have to work; that unmanageable bunch of teenagers who are always making too much racket; the pastor or that trustee who always seems to rub you the wrong way. Either these are dead ends or divine opportunities. Only the Spirit will help you see these may be open doors.

4. Now move toward one of these doors, praying as you go. Test it; you may see it swing wide open. Christ has been there all the time waiting for you to join Him on the other side.

5. You will discover allies who have been waiting for someone to make the first move. People who will ask questions or drop comments revealing their feelings of dissatisfaction, but also of hope. "Perhaps something could be done to

change this." Invite them to join you, not to criticize or complain, but to become a ministering team, a task force for the Lord.

6. Share the story. Let the congregation know what you are seeing the Lord do, as Paul and Barnabas did when they came back to home base at Antioch with a glowing report of the wondrous things the Lord was doing among the Gentiles. That can have a renewing effect on all the people. "This church is coming alive!"

7. Know that you are free to fail! We learn more from our disappointments than from our victories. Take stock, regroup, and press on in the power of the Lord.

Chapter   Four

A Party at Matthew's House

*"And as He sat at table in the house,
behold, many tax collectors and sinners came
and sat down with Jesus and His disciples."*
Matthew 9:10

I grew up in a home that breathed a concern for those "out-side Christ." So it was natural for my name to be high on the list of those for whom my parents prayed with great fervor. There was great rejoicing when I went forward to publicly confess I wanted to be a Christian shortly after my tenth birthday. On a cold December night, after hearing a visiting evangelist give a passionate message on the Lost Sheep, I knew I was "that sheep." I have never known any guilt more painful or personal than I experienced that night. When the invitation was given I whispered to my friend Delbert Gustafson, "I'm going up there." When he answered, "I'm going with you," at least I knew I would have company. What a long walk it was to the front, although we were seated only three rows back. But at any age, that journey is never short. I remember how joyfully my father greeted me in the inquiry room. When he asked, "Why did you come tonight, Roger?" I could only answer, "Because I want to go to heaven." Our tears of gratitude were joined in prayer.

The lunch my mother served after the meeting was a holy, hilarious affair—really a sacramental time which is vividly etched in my mind after more than fifty years. I felt so liberated and clean.

There was no way I could hold back what had happened. So the next day as we were leaving our one-room country school for home, I blurted out the good news to my fourth-grade friend Roy Lundberg. And then I asked him if he had ever "let Jesus into his heart." After all, weren't Christians supposed to share Jesus? I was somewhat taken aback when he said he didn't know what that meant. So in the only way a ten-year-old boy can do it, I tried to explain how he could really know Jesus as his Saviour.

That evening my father received an angry call from this boy's father. "Your son had no business talking to my boy that way. Doesn't he know that we are loyal members of the Center Lutheran Church?" He was a man to be reckoned with, for he was on the school board. But my father brushed it off, saying he was proud I had "spoken a word for Jesus so soon."

That was the beginning of my "evangelistic endeavor." And through the years that concern to "share Jesus" has never left me. Sometimes burning like a fire, and at other times cool and diffused, it is always there, whether expressed or hidden, a restless longing to reach someone for Christ, like a haunting, unfinished melody. I have not deserved this concern, nor have I earned it. It is a gift! And now and then Paul's urgent word to the Corinthians, "Woe to me if I preach not the Gospel," has brought me up short, reminding me again of this inescapable calling. And to this day I am deeply stirred whenever I hear those familiar words from the old Gospel hymn, "Care for the erring ones, lift up the fallen."

That calling was refreshed and sharpened during my sophomore year in college. I remember very little about that service in Central Baptist one October Sunday morning, except the verse Gordon Hasselblad used as a basis for his message, "I am crucified with Christ: nevertheless I live; yet not I, but Christ liveth in me: and the life which I now live in the flesh I live by the faith of the Son of God, who loved me, and gave Himself for me" (Galatians 2:20, KJV). Once again I could not resist the call. It was a moment of fresh surrender to Jesus as

Lord after a period of spiritual carelessness and wandering.

At the conclusion of that service Eric Swanson, a humble, devoted servant of the Lord who made his living as a wholesale clothing salesman, took me home for Sunday dinner. After I had stuffed myself on his wife's delicious Swedish cooking, he announced, "Now we will go to the county jail for a service. That will be a good place for you to start, Roger. After some singing you can share a word of testimony with the men in one of the cell blocks." No ifs, ands, or buts. That was it. All I could do was go along and nervously join the little band at the Minnehaha County Jail. After singing half a dozen Gospel songs, the five of us each went to a different cell block to share a word of witness.

Half scared to death, I faced a few men, mostly disinterested, some washing their clothes, others playing cards, probably wondering what this young kid was trying to pull off talking about, "God is no respecter of persons." That was the best I could come up with on such short notice. But somehow I survived, and left with a sense of quiet elation. And that was only the beginning!

Most of that year I joined Eric and his group every Sunday at the jail, helped set up the little organ, joined in some hymns, and then with Bible in hand would try to utter a few words with anyone who would listen. It was a stretching, growing experience. Eric Swanson was far more of a mentor than he ever realized. For as I watched that loving man faithfully leading out in this unsung ministry week after week, my passion to reach straying, needy sinners for Christ was again kindled. It seemed Eric worked all week so he could have the privilege of coming to that jail on Sundays to share Christ with those men.

There came a day when a younger man, behind bars for passing bad checks, confessed that booze had been his downfall. He was reaching out for help. "How can I get out of this mess and start over?" Almost frantically I looked around for someone I could call on for help. But no one was available. So I had to strike out on my own, green and inexperienced as I was. All I could do was share a bit of my own story, and even though my worldly knowledge at that time was quite limited, he listened as if his life depended on it. Then I did quote John 3:16, using his name, Cliff, in place of "world" and "whosoever." A message of hope not only for Cliff but for me!

As I spoke those old, old words I became strangely aware that Cliff's time had come. I could see it in his eyes. So with sweaty hands I drew a deep breath—the question is too crucial to be put casually—and said it, "Cliff, maybe this is your time. Christ is the only one who can help you start over. Why don't you take a chance on Him?" In the years since, I have never raised that question without that same kind of excited wonder. "Is this the right time?"

Cliff's answer that day was so affirmative and immediate I was taken by surprise. "That's what I want. How do I do it?" "Cliff, you talk to Him. He's your friend. Just tell Christ you're thankful He died for you. Ask Him to forgive your sins and tell Him you believe in Him and trust Him as your Lord and Saviour. I'll pray first. Then you follow." He nodded his head. "Go ahead." So I somewhat breathlessly asked the Lord to help Cliff pray to receive Him just as he was. Then he simply and haltingly voiced what was on his heart. "I've never done this before, but I want to try. Lord, You know how much I've sinned. Will You forgive me? I want Jesus to be my Saviour. Thanks for dying for me." When Cliff lifted his head, his face was radiant with joy. That jail cell was filled with the glory of God.

I left with my heart singing. I had been present at a spiritual birth, a mysterious, eternal transaction, and I marveled that the Spirit could use my amateurish, hesitant efforts in guiding, convicting, and converting as He did. The wonder of that first experience has never left me.

Over the years I have continued to be amazed as I have witnessed an incredible assortment of folks being given "power to become children of God . . . born, not of blood nor of the will of the flesh nor of the will of man, but of God" (John 1:12-13). A few of those names and places come to mind. Not only in churchly settings, but on a United Airlines flight between Calgary, Canada, and Denver; on a used car lot in Sioux Falls; in a college locker room in Ottawa; on a street corner in Kansas City; in a halfway house for ex-convicts; in the Petroleum Club in Wichita; at a kitchen table in a Sioux Falls suburban home; under a tree at Green Lake, Wisconsin; in the Broadview Hotel in Wichita; and time after time in the pastor's study. Each time I have been filled anew with the joy and privilege of the evangelistic calling.

But how could that passion for seeking the lost be kindled in an old, mainline church in downtown Wichita? Particularly when years of struggle had sapped the church of much of its spiritual initiative. In fact, I found myself both saddened and perplexed when people would speak of Chet Fadley, almost as if he were some kind of an exhibit. He was the one person who had confessed Christ and been baptized during those years when the congregation was not meeting in its own building at Second and Broadway. And in those early months of our ministry at First Baptist, week after week would go by with no one taking an open stand for Christ whenever the call was issued. It was particularly disturbing that people seemed to accept this as the normal state of affairs.

But there was no way I could quicken an urgency to bring the lost to Christ among these dear people through my own strength or ingenuity. Evangelistic sermons without end, however eloquent, would not create that burning concern. Neither would some new high-powered scheme to motivate the people, whether by fear or guilt or reward, send them out to bring in the unreached.

No, if anything were to happen it must be God's doing, the work of the Spirit. Had not the risen Christ "charged them not to depart from Jerusalem, but to wait for the promise of the Father"? Then, "You shall receive power when the Holy Spirit has come upon you; and you shall be my witnesses in Jerusalem and in all Judea and Samaria and to the ends of the earth" (Acts 1:4, 8). This was not an option but a spiritual mandate—not only for those early believers, but also for twentieth-century believers in Wichita, Kansas.

But were we willing to wait expectantly to receive that power? And how? That meant changing our agenda. Expectant, believing prayer must be at the center of all our dreams and hopes and ministry. No longer could we make our plans and then stick on a little prayer at the end expecting the Lord to bless us. It would be only when the risen Lord had "breathed on us" that we would be sent out in power as the Father had sent the Son.

So we began to quietly call our people to prayer. Not just that the Lord would enlarge our work, but that we might hunger after Him and know Him. We asked that He would flood us with His life and Spirit, giving us a longing to reach the lost and straying. And we grew in this, moving little by little beyond perfunctory, almost rote, prayers to more open, free utterances of praise and petition.

We encouraged people to join in a prayer vigil, a beautiful procession of folks coming and going every half hour for twenty-four hours, kneeling in the tiny chapel to pour out their hearts in confession and praise and petition. More and more we sought to saturate our services of worship, our staff meetings, our committee and board meetings, and our church planning sessions with prayer. Now and then we would pause in the regular flow of business to give thanks or lift up a need. At first this seemed a bit strange for some, but later they joined in.

And we began to pray with new earnestness for people's needs. The specific prayer requests written on the "friendship cards" in morning worship—often thirty or more—were shared in staff meetings and in a couple of small prayer groups, and were then sent out to six homebound folks who were volunteer "prayer warriors." On a couple of occasions the church staff spent a morning praying for every member listed in our directory and also for scores of unreached people whose names came to mind. What began as the whisper of a handful in a corner became more and more an open chorus, a congregation uniting in prayer.

Guests were invited to come and teach us about the mystery and power of prayer. Ray and Anne Ortlund, recently of Lake Avenue Congregational Church in Pasadena, dealt with the cost and joy of spiritual surrender; Carl and Nancy Lundquist, who had spent most of a year visiting retreat centers, led us in the deepening of the inner life; Philip Hinerman, Art Erickson, and Eddie Thomas, serving as a team in an old inner-city congregation in Minneapolis which by all human standards should have died, spoke with authority about the visitation of the Spirit that had renewed their people. And Richard Foster, author of *Celebration of Discipline*, spent most of a day with fifty of our people. Evelyn Christensen shared a day with almost 400 women from the community instructing them in *What Happens When Women Pray*. Three prayer groups in our congregation were spontaneously drawn together as an outgrowth of that day.

This did not bring any kind of sudden spiritual breakthrough, but we could sense quiet, almost imperceptible changes in our life together. We were being given a deepened sense of love and concern for one another, a joy in simply being together. People began to linger after the services, not wanting to leave each other. Certainly the Lord was pleased to hear the soft sounds of their laughter and conversation or the prayers of some who would occasionally gather in little clusters to lift up a concern. And the people were beginning to help one another in simple ways — getting together to repair someone's leaky roof, or giving a hand when a fellow member had to move, or caring for a sick child. Often someone would speak openly about sharing Christ with a member of the family or a neighbor.

Worship seemed to be coming alive. People were entering the sanctuary with new expectancy, some even bowing to pray before the service began, singing the hymns more lustily, and participating openly in our times of family prayer. And what a joy to hear the quiet rustle of Bibles being opened at the time of the sermon. The Spirit was drawing us together, teaching us to be "kind to one another, tenderhearted, forgiving one another, as God in Christ forgave you" (Ephesians 4:32). And this deepened, renewed spirit among us was crucial, for spiritual reproduction is the inevitable result of healthy body life.

Of course, evangelism is personal, "one beggar sharing bread he has found with a fellow beggar." But it is no lone-ranger undertaking, not a private enterprise carried on outside of or alien to the family of God. We have become far too conformed to a worldly, rugged American individualistic style of evangelism. So much of it is a programmed one-on-one "quick sell," getting someone to "sign the card," then toting up another statistic after the prospect has "prayed the sinner's prayer." Too often that new convert is left to struggle on alone, isolated and vulnerable, unrelated to any growing, loving body of believers. This is not a New Testament model of evangelism.

And we have been reaping the fruits of this lone-ranger soul saving—long lists of inactive members; spiritual babes who died at birth, never discipled nor made accountable to any body of believers; self-centered churches full of unsubmissive, carnal members—"I'm leaving. I don't like the way you're doing things here"; people church shopping, like switching channels on TV, always trying to find the right program; a consumer religion—"Jesus will take care of all your needs"—that shuns costly discipleship. Success and prosperity are guaranteed.

Is it any wonder that forty to fifty million Americans who claim to be "born-again believers" make little or no impact on public policy and seem powerless to transform the growing secularism of the marketplace and the church?

No, evangelism is a ministry of the body, an act of spiritual reproduction, being born into the community of believers. After Luke writes about the quality of life given to the early, emerging church by the Spirit—"apostles' teaching and fellowship, breaking of bread and the prayers . . . distributing to any that had need . . . praising God . . . wonders and signs"— then he adds, "And the Lord added to their number day by day those who were being saved" (Acts 2:42-47). How could any needy seeker resist the joy and spontaneity of that living community?

We are inviting people to enter into Christ who dwells among His people. The head and the body are inseparable, as are the "groom and the bride," the "chief cornerstone and the living building." One theologian has called this "the whole Christ." Here is where we teach the new believers, nourish them, equip them, model for them the kingdom style of life. *Evangelism cannot be divorced from the quality of life in the congregation.* It is the joy and freedom we have come to know in belonging to Christ and His people which compels us to eagerly invite others into the family.

Yet the established, institutional church can become a caricature of the real thing. New believers often come so hopeful and eager, not understanding how dirty and smelly it can be "inside the ark." They don't expect this crowd to be so competitive and critical, so uptight and overprogrammed. How could the so-called "people of God" be such an ingrown, stuffy social club? And often they feel the resentment of the old-timers: "Why should 'they' come in here and act as if they owned the place? Don't they know we've been around here a long time holding this place together?" So the new believers may draw back and go elsewhere, or lose interest and end up on the inactive roll, finally giving up on the church in disappointed anger. As Sam Shoemaker, that creative churchman, said so long ago, "Most churches wouldn't know what to do with a red-hot convert. It would be like putting a live chick under a dead hen."

But how different in a living congregation. Here the Spirit in a mysterious but very real way communicates reality. An invitation deeper than words is being issued, not simply by mere humans, who at best are forgiven sinners, as they speak the words of Scripture or prayer, song or preaching. It is an invitation from Christ Himself, who dwells among these people, who makes Himself known not only through those words of worship, but also through the acts of baptism and the Lord's Supper, through moments of silence or the warm greeting of a fellow worshiper, but most deeply through the love He has shed abroad in drawing the congregation together. "By this all men will know that you are My disciples, if you have love for one another" (John 13:35).

Then that lonely, guilt-ridden, rebellious, anxious, even presumably self-sufficient person is touched and addressed at the center of his or her life. A longing is kindled, a hunger awakened, causing that person to wonder, "What's so different about these people? Why do I feel so restless and empty, even so emotional?" but not knowing at that moment that this is the Spirit at work, unseen but ever-present, calling, convicting, and converting. So we were delighted and praised God for every stirring of new life among the people in Wichita.

One of the signs of that stirring was the way our people received Anna Grissom, one of the more interesting characters from our neighborhood. How well I remember her striding into the church the first time with her frizzy gray hair and an angry, troubled look in her deep-set eyes. She desperately needed help, but was too proud to admit it at first, covering it up with talk, but eventually letting it leak out. So our people gave her a bit of food and some rent money, with a large dose of love thrown in, assuming we wouldn't see her again.

But Anna began showing up for the Wednesday evening fellowship suppers and Sunday morning worship, usually coming late or leaving early, making certain that people wouldn't miss her presence.

Every now and then I would find a sealed envelope addressed to "The Reverend" on my desk containing a barely legible note scribbled on cheap paper, sometimes a beautiful, childlike expression of thanks, other times spewing anger. Often a quarter or a dollar bill would be attached, her attempt to pay back what had been shared with her as a gift. These notes were signed either "From a friend," or "Guess you don't know who wrote this." Then she would later ask, "Did you find something on your desk?" Her phone calls to our

home, usually during the evening meal, were that way too—
either angry, "I'm never coming back to that church again,"
or tender, "I don't know what I'd do without you folks."

As Anna began to trust us, knowing we weren't going to
reject her regardless of how she acted, she began to open her
life a bit. Two of her sons by an earlier marriage, Clarence
and Roy, were longtime inmates at the State Penitentiary in
Lansing, one of them in maximum security. Occasionally
Anna would share a pathetic, self-pitying letter from Roy. Her
daughter had been in and out of alcoholic treatment for years,
and another son wandered the streets of Wichita or mooched
off his mother while he drifted from one job to another.

One day in a moment of rare candor, Anna spoke of seeing
an older brother kill himself. She described vividly how she
had seen him come rushing out of the bathroom with blood
gushing out of his throat after slashing himself with a broken
bottle. He stumbled and bled to death on the kitchen floor.
Anna was nine years old at the time, and had been haunted
by that traumatic scene ever since.

But the people at First Baptist did not turn away from her
or ignore her. Although she was a loner, they accepted her
for what she was. I quietly praised God for the way the
Crescent Philathea Sunday School Class, a strong group of
women, most of them longtime members of the church, welcomed and included her. Socially and emotionally there was a
great gulf between Anna and most of our people, but in
Christ, where there is "neither Jew nor Greek, neither slave
nor free, neither male nor female," that chasm was bridged
long ago. So Anna discovered she was no longer an outsider,
but was being brought near by the One "who is our peace."

The day came when Anna could no longer hold back. The
constraint of the Spirit was greater than all her fears. There
was a look of fierce determination on her face as she came
striding forward, this time to declare her allegiance to Christ.
She was willing to risk being accepted by this family, and that
trust was not misplaced. The people received Anna as a sister
in Christ.

But that was not the last time she "came forward." For every four or five months she would make that journey to the front, drawn, it seemed, mostly by her needs and her longing to once again be affirmed. "Do these people still know I'm here? Will they continue to accept me even though I feel so unworthy?" Each time I would greet her with whatever words the Spirit gave me. "This is our friend and sister in Christ, Anna Grissom, renewing her vows with Christ and this family. Thank God she is here. She is a part of our life. We pray that the Lord will give Anna His strength as she faces the struggles of each day. I'm sure many of you will want to greet her after the benediction."

As I would speak words such as these, I could not help being aware of what the eyes and body language of our people seemed to be saying. Never once did I detect a spirit of rejection, "Why is she doing this again?" But I saw understanding and acceptance. What a joy then to watch people bless and encourage Anna after the service, not condescendingly, but with grace and warmth.

And so it was that Bob and Patty Neff, who had been observing all this as visitors, felt drawn to join our congregation. Ruth and I loved them as neighbors and fellow Christians, and often enjoyed their enthusiastic hospitality, particularly when they encouraged us to use their swimming pool whenever our granddaughters came to visit. But I was reluctant to presume on their kindness by asking them "if they didn't want to join our church," even though they had been worshiping with us for some months.

However, they surprised me as I greeted them at the door one Sunday by asking, "When are you coming by to visit with us about the church?" I had wrongly assumed they would eventually join where their close friends attended, particularly their tennis-playing partners.

That was all I needed to hear. That week I walked over to visit them. After some pleasantries I came to the point. "Why would you dear people even consider joining First Baptist when so many of your friends are active in other churches?

And look at the distance you have to travel to get down to First Baptist." Patty was very honest. "I must confess I never thought I'd ever end up being a Baptist, and that sanctuary simply intimidates me." But Bob's answer said it all, "We want to be a part of a church that treats people the way First Baptist treats Anna. I guess that's why we're drawn to the church." I walked home singing. An invitation had been extended through an accepting, caring congregation. The next Sunday Bob and Patty came to join our family.

Or there was Rosa Christison, an attractive younger businesswoman who came to see me. I sensed a deep pain in her. Yes, she confessed, she was troubled. A meaningful relationship had come to an end just as her job was being eliminated in a company shakeup. Now she was struggling with discouragement. "Where is God in all this?" She had visited First Baptist the previous Sunday at the urging of a friend. As she put it ever so softly, struggling to control her emotions, "I debated about coming and finally decided to give it a try. When I walked into this place I was almost overwhelmed by the huge sanctuary and I felt more alone than ever. When you asked people to greet one another, I didn't know if I dared move toward anyone. So I just stood there. Then a wonderful thing happened. An older woman who reminded me of my grandmother came over, introduced herself, and asked my name. Then she asked, 'Would you mind if I sat with you during worship?' It was like coming home. I could not hold back the tears." Again, there were gentle tears on Rosa's face.

I then tried to explain. "Rosa, when that dear woman came to be with you that was God's way of saying, 'I will never leave you alone.'" So we visited about the meaning of Christ and His family and she left somewhat reassured and a bit more hopeful.

There were other ups and downs. One visit did not mean the end of the struggles. But in the end Rosa gave herself to Christ anew. I shall never forget the light on Rosa's face the day she was baptized, reflecting beautifully the glory of

Christ. Why? Someone, moved by the Spirit, had obeyed and dared reach out to discover a lonely, needy friend. No way could that be humanly programmed, but surely it was an answer to prayer.

And that's the way it was when Dick Coe greeted Gary Ayers so casually in the narthex, just before worship. "Isn't this your first time here? Well, I'm glad you're here. I'm Dick Coe and this is my wife, Debbie. We'd love to have you sit with us during worship." How utterly simple and natural but, oh, the consequence of that timely invitation!

Gary was a promising, younger attorney in a large, well-known downtown law firm, one of those people in whom the Lord had invested at least five talents. He was a free spirit, and somewhat lonely, because his wife, Charleen, a gifted soloist, was spending a year at Yale University getting her master's degree in voice. She was there on a prestigious scholarship studying under Phyllis Curtin, who had formerly taught Beverly Sills—an opportunity not to be turned down. So Gary and Charleen were seeing each other only in snatches every five or six weeks.

When Charleen came home for Christmas all of us were delighted and surprised when she and Gary came forward asking to be members of the First Baptist family. It was the second Sunday the two of them had worshiped with us together. And what joy and life these two shared with our people, not as prima donnas, which they could have easily done, but as humble servants of the Lord. Not only through heartwarming, lifting music, but in opening their home to all kinds of people or in joining our young people on their skiing trips, or in giving inspired leadership to one of our newly married classes.

Many of us have had the day brightened by Gary's unique sense of humor. I remember receiving a copy of an announcement he had sent out to the Koinonia Class announcing the upcoming lesson. His closing word was, "In the event the rapture takes place before we meet next week, Pastor Roger will teach the class for those who remain."

All this because Dick Coe had been obedient to the impulse of the Spirit. Gary later spoke of that invitation. "The tears welled up when Dick spoke so warmly. I didn't realize how deeply I was yearning for someone to notice me in church, even speak to me. I had experienced so many disappointments in visiting other churches since coming back to Wichita. No one seemed to even know I was there. So I was wondering if I dared give First Baptist a try. The Tuesday noon Bible study luncheon I had attended there the previous week had seemed like a friendly, open affair. I wondered if the worship could be the same. But if I was ignored again I didn't know how long it would be before I would go back to any church." So Gary came reluctantly but hopefully. And that small risk was rewarded.

The Lord has a marvelous sense of timing, for Dick Coe had only recently been given the grace to become an "inviter" for the Lord. Bright and articulate, he was obviously a comer in financial affairs, holding a prominent position for seven years in Continental Bank in Chicago. He was enjoying the good life in the fast lane as a swinging bachelor, so he thought, until the Lord outflanked him.

It started in a Lenten series at Fourth Presbyterian Church in Chicago through a neighborhood group of young adults studying Catherine Marshall's book *Beyond Ourselves*. Everything went along fine until Dick came to the twelfth chapter which deals with "ego-slaying." Here Catherine quoted Jesus, "Whosoever will save his life shall lose it, but whosoever shall lose his life for my sake . . . shall save it" (Mark 8:35, KJV). Then she went on to say, "To put it another way, there is no solution apart from the painful, all-out one of handing over to Him all of our natural self to be destroyed . . . so that Christ can give us a new self, one born from above, one in which He will be at the center of our being."[1] As Dick put it, "That started to make me uncomfortable. I already had a few problems, and I didn't need any more." The class had now become more than an interesting intellectual exercise. In all his church experience Dick had never dealt with the central claim of the Living Christ.

The generous paycheck at the bank, his loving parents, his attractive girlfriend, and all his interesting friends were not enough. Where was it all taking him? What was really the purpose of his life? So Dick quietly and thoughtfully surrendered it all to Christ, gave Him all the keys to his life. As he said later, "This is really the only way to go."

And then he came home to Wichita in January of 1978 to sort it all out. He showed up at the church, after plans to work for a friend in a political campaign fell through, saying, "I want to learn and grow in Christ. Can I follow you around, visit with you, do some reading, and help out wherever possible?" So for the next few months this is what Dick did. And what a challenge it was having this new friend join me in an informal discipling relationship. He often asked, "Why did you say or do that?" after we had made a pastoral call or visited with someone about Christ, or come out of a staff meeting. Which made me wonder too. And I was refreshed by some of our searching discussions after he had literally devoured one of the books dealing with discipleship or church renewal I had recommended he read.

Dick willingly took on some of the lowly tasks which are always a part of church ministry, even driving a troubled, loquacious alcoholic to Valley Hope at Norton, Kansas. He returned home quite exhausted after that eight-hour trip with a character quite different from the Continental Bank clientele.

His greatest frustration may well have been that his valiant attempts to get me better organized met with only very modest success. However, our frequent times of prayer together were rich and deep. He will always be a spiritual son.

Eventually Dick found his vocational fulfillment in insurance and financial planning, for him a deeply pastoral "tentmaking" ministry. Then he discovered he had a calling and gift in discipling other men and in drawing together small Bible study and prayer groups. Then he met and came to love Debbie. Their whole wedding experience—rehearsal, prenuptial dinner, and the service itself—was one of the most uniquely beautiful expressions of what God intended Christian marriage to be I have ever witnessed. People, ever since, have said, "We want a wedding like that." To which I have responded, "You can if you pay the price of that kind of commitment." And like the disciple Andrew, Dick has been faithfully extending that intriguing invitation, "Come and see."

We cannot simply hope to reach people for Christ on our turf, within the confines of the sanctuary. For there are all those people in the thick of life, "outside the gate," who do not feel at home in a church building with the "holy crowd." They are often fearful they do not have the right clothes or know the "in" language, and are certain they simply are not good enough. How often have I heard people say, "I just don't feel at home in that kind of thing." These are our neighbors, members of our family, fellow-workers, or friends in our social circles. People in our "social networks," to use Lyle Schaller's phrase, often have deeper longings and needs than we ever realized.

Jesus met people on their turf, not in the synagogue or the temple. There He confronted them, revealing His identity to them, challenging them to accept His gift of life.

I have been intrigued by Matthew's understated account of his decision to follow Jesus. The invitation came to him at his tax collector's box. He describes his own response in strong, imperative language, "and he rose and followed Him" (Matthew 9:9). Then he called his friends together for a dinner party, eager for them to meet this amazing Man who had begun to change the whole direction of his life. How else could he explain giving up his lucrative tax business?

It has been well documented that most of the fresh, uninhibited witnessing for Christ is done in the first two years after one's conversion. Then we become domesticated, join committees, and get busy doing church work. Our ardor cools as we become more theoretical and tentative. We are now in the religious ghetto and we no longer speak that unashamed, enthusiastic word for Christ. This never did happen to Matthew, who much later in his Christian experience gave us his Gospel.

And who were these friends Matthew invited to his party? Not the religious crowd, the scribes and Pharisees. No, it was the people who belonged to his "social network." Many "tax collectors and sinners," a bunch of cheating outcasts. But these were the people he knew. And where was the party? Not in the "temple fellowship hall," but at his home, probably a fairly fancy place considering the kind of money he had been making.

Here Jesus "sat at table in the house," not on the edge, but right in the middle of things, chatting and laughing, enjoying the food and the company. This was no grim, tight-lipped affair but a joyous "salvation party." After all, Matthew had been liberated.

For the religious crowd, this whole affair was obscene and vulgar. What kind of a Teacher was this who could enjoy Himself with this dirty, sinful party? Ah, but it was these "bad characters," these who really knew they were sick, who welcomed Jesus so eagerly. While those self-righteous critics, so utterly convinced they had no need of a physician, turned their backs on Him and missed the life and healing Jesus could have shared with them.

How much we have to learn from Jesus who had no cut-and-dried "evangelistic program." He compassionately and freely entered the world of the spiritually ill wherever He found them—at a well or in a tree, on the street or in a home, at a wedding or a funeral—and there shared His saving grace.

As I meditated on this, I began to wonder why we couldn't have "parties at Matthew's house" with "Jesus sitting at table with us"? Have people come together in a comfortable, relaxed setting where they could meet new friends and hear Jesus talked about in a casual, but very honest, way? Why not ride in on an American way of socializing where people seemed to stand around at every kind of gathering chatting or carrying on business with a coffee cup or a cocktail glass in hand? We could combine this with Jesus' free style of moving so easily among the unreached and simply call them "house parties." Then perhaps seeking, interested friends might have a taste of authentic community in a nonthreatening home setting and also discover that Jesus was for real, the One who had come to heal us.

So I threw out this idea at the next Board meeting, hoping for a positive response. I had hardly finished before they were saying, "Let's give it a try." And before the meeting was over we had more homes offered for "house parties" than we could possibly handle.

Our first party turned out to be a hilarious, loving affair, going beyond our fondest hopes. People hardly wanted to leave for home. Surely the Spirit was in this. That party was only the foretaste of all that was to come in these spiritual serendipities over the years. For eventually we were having one every four to six weeks and at least seventy-five percent of all the people who committed themselves to Christ and His church in the next years came by way of these parties. They became, to use another of Lyle Schaller's phrases, "ports of entry."

How important it was to find hosts with the gift of hospitality, who could greet people warmly, "Welcome. We're Bob and Patty, and we're so glad you've come to our home. Now what are your names again? Let us take your wraps. Could we get you a cup of coffee or a cool drink and a cookie?" The "newcomers" had been invited either by one of our lay folk or a staff person, usually someone they knew, and often brought by the one inviting them.

Then after the folks had arrived and were mingling, we would encourage them to go to someone they did not know, introduce themselves to each other, find out "what you do," and at least "one interesting thing about yourself." While this was going on chairs would be brought in. People who had been on the "cocktail circuit" taught me that a new crowd always mingles best standing with a cup or glass in hand. Sitting in chairs nervously looking at one another can be deadly. As these introductions were then made, we always had a lot of good laughs but also some unexpected tender moments as we came to know a bit about one another.

Then I would usually initiate a time of sharing around the circle asking each one to answer a simple question, "What are you specifically thankful for tonight?" or, "Name a person who has deeply influenced your life," or "What is one of the best things that has happened to you this week?" It might take forty-five minutes or an hour to get around the circle. And what intimate, often tender or humorous, experiences and memories this simple exercise would unlock. Which many times prompted someone to speak a fresh, unrehearsed word for Christ. A contagious power seemed to be let loose by the very honesty and spontaneity of such a confession. I recall at least two occasions when a person in the circle simply blurted out a longing to become a Christian. Each time people gathered round in loving, prayerful support as this person entered the kingdom in repentance and faith.

Then we would express our hope that everyone present might have experienced the kind of spirit which we longed to have characterize our congregational life. We have never labeled who was "in" and who was "out" at these parties, but encouraged those interested to seek any of us out for further help or to check out our membership class. The evening would usually conclude with a round of song, a time of gentle harmony, and finally the passing of a blessing around the circle.

It was to one of these parties that Al and Mary Sue Ford came, an evening filled with laughter and surprises, at the home of Lyman and Helen Huber, longtime faithful members who enjoyed themselves more than anyone else when they got beyond their initial nervousness. As we were leaving Al quietly asked, "Could I come by and see you some time?" He was a man's man who had spent most of his life at Christopher Steel. No way he would ask to meet with a preacher unless he were deadly serious about something. I immediately responded, "You name the time, Al, and I'll be there."

When a request comes with that kind of intensity, all other appointments are secondary. Surely he was eager, because he came right back, "How about tomorrow?" We agreed to meet at 2:00 P.M.

Al and Mary Sue had first shown up at First Baptist some weeks earlier when their daughter, Jancy, was baptized. She had become a believer at Ottawa University. I remember how excited she was that day. "I'm so happy. My dad and mom are here today." Al later reported, "I went out one of the side doors after the service so I wouldn't have to greet you. I didn't want anyone to see how emotional I was about the whole thing." The next Saturday he almost off-handedly asked, "How would you like to go to church tomorrow, Mary Sue?" All she could say was, "Al, I've waited twenty-five years for you to say that," trying to hide her excitement. So they began attending worship at First Baptist, now leaving by "my door," so I came to know who they were. Eventually we invited them to the Hubers for a house party.

When Al came to my office that afternoon, he had barely gotten in the door when he asked, "Well, how do you begin?" No point in putting it off. That's why he had come! And I said, "On your knees, Al." And that's what that strong man did—dropped to his knees. I could only join him with a New Testament in hand, explaining simply how we all start with Christ—in repentance and childlike trust—and sharing a Scripture verse here and there. He understood and prayed. His halting, fervent words opened the floodgates of grace. As we stood and embraced, now brothers in the Spirit, the warm glow on Al's face reflected the light of Christ.

That was only the beginning. Al and Mary Sue's baptism turned out to be a glorious evangelistic event. Not only did Jancy's husband, Mike, join them, but members of their family were on hand witnessing their confession of faith. I particularly remember meeting Al's mother, Ruth, that day, a woman of gentle dignity, well into her seventies, who introduced me to others in the family. Some weeks later leaving church Ruth said, "Aren't you getting tired of having me attend your church as a visitor?" At first I misunderstood. Then I realized that she too wanted to confess Christ. When we visited in her home later in the week I became aware how eager she was to follow Christ. That day she too became a believer, and was eager to be baptized in spite of her age and defective eyesight. How well I remember removing the glasses of this nervous but determined woman some weeks later as she stood in the baptismal waters. And I also recall that wondrous look of quiet triumph as she arose from the watery grave. The Lord had truly blessed her with His Spirit in this act of obedience.

Then it was Ginny Collom, Al's sister, who shared at another house party how her high school daughter Sally, newly converted, had confronted her. "Mother, do you really know if you're saved or not?" Ginny said, "I answered her 'Yes' somewhat timidly, knowing immediately I had not spoken the truth." Her guilt, the convicting work of the Spirit, had driven Ginny to her knees in the early morning hours. Here she asked Christ to take over. And was given a peace she had never known before. She too was baptized. Some weeks later her husband, Byron, whom we always called "B," was restored to Christ and joined the family of God.

Then it was Dee Ann, Al and Mary Sue's other daughter, coming out of her loneliness and need to find new life in Christ. And finally their son, Fred, home from Kansas State, who said, "I've been a Christian since high school days, but I've never belonged to a church. Now I want to join my family and this body in baptism." In fact, it was his witness much earlier, as a member of the Fellowship of Christian Athletes, that had been the first seed the Lord had sown in the life of his parents.

So one life had touched another until most of an entire family had entered the kingdom. Has this not always been Christ's best way? "Andrew first found his brother Simon, and said to him, 'We have found the Messiah' . . . He brought him to Jesus" (John 1:41-42).

But evangelism is also a door-to-door ministry, going out to meet people in their homes, sharing with them there God's word of "Shalom." We are to go as the seventy were sent, lambs among wolves, without excess baggage. Whenever the door is opened our first word, like theirs, is to be, "Peace to this house." We come with a message of healing and reconciliation. Neither the message nor the strategy has changed.

And that mission has not been given to a select committee or some specialized handful, but to all the people of God. But how to find who will go? These callers, door-to-door lay evangelists, will not respond to public appeals, but must be sought out and invited, and trained for the task. Lay people will discover the joy of sharing the Good News person to person in some home only through experience. No class on evangelism, however carefully taught, or instructional manual will ever be a substitute for "getting into the trenches," going out and doing it. But how, unless we take them by the hand and walk them through the whole experience, step by step?

Was this not the strategy of Jesus? Taking a handful of men — a nondescript lot, but diamonds in the rough — and sharing with them the style of kingdom life. This He did by teaching, but also by modeling for them by word and deed how the kingdom was to be proclaimed. He did it by taking them on retreats, answering their questions, then sending them out on field trips and carefully checking them out when they returned. No careless, slipshod discipling with Him. So it was with the Apostle Paul, who taught Luke and Timothy, Silas and Epaphras, and all the other fellow travelers in the heat of the mission. No armchair theorizing with him.

So over the years I have sought out men to join me in the adventure of evangelistic calling. Strong men, who have the gift of speaking a word for Christ, but often buried beneath their fears and inexperience. A gift waiting to be "called forth." Why cannot men who are handling heavy responsibilities in their work and in the community be enlisted to join Christ in His "big business"? Getting beyond carrying pledge cards or ushering or serving on some committee, to enter homes and there issue the invitation in His behalf?

As we have prayed and called together, these men have watched me struggle, make mistakes, endure a bit of humiliation now and then, but have also listened to me pose the question, "Have you ever thought of giving yourself to Christ?" And finally I have encouraged them to "go it on their own," then to find someone to join them in enlarging the mission. There is a contagion about this that begins to affect a congregation.

So in Wichita there were men who joined me in this venture whom I will carry in my heart all the days of my life — Ed Friesen, George Morgan, Bruce Middleton, Roger Fraley, Bob Neff, Charlie Schultz, and Bob Kitchen who often would drive home 180 miles from Oklahoma City where he was involved in construction work to be on hand for our Tuesday night calling. And there are others!

But there is one among these who stands out, Glen Holman, a gentle, caring man who was always eager to "make the call." Often on Sunday Glen would ask, "What time do you want me to pick you up this week?" God had uniquely prepared him for this ministry. He had been a sales supervisor for a coffee company for most of his working years, often responsible for twenty or more sales people, trying to please a demanding boss.

Glen had come forward in response to the invitation some years earlier because he thought "this was the right thing to do," for the sake of his wife, Alice, and their two sons, Don and Gerry. That day their pastor had simply announced, "You'll be baptized tonight." So Glen went through the motions and, as he later put it, had "rattled around the church for twenty-one years, not knowing what it was all about." "During those years," he said, "I wore two sets of shoes, one for Sunday and another for the rest of the week, and had two kinds of language, church talk on Sunday and tough, swearing talk the rest of the week."

Finally the pressures at work got so bad Glen came to the end of his resources, starting for work some days with devastating headaches and sometimes even vomiting. Then one day on his way to work, dreading it all, the darkness and pain closed in on him with such power he pulled his car to the curb and simply cried out, "Lord, I can't run this show any more. You've got to take over." That desperate plea from the pit was the turning point. Little by little, light and freedom began to flood his life. Glen became God's man. He now came to see the needs of his boss. He was given a new, clean speech for every day of the week. Best of all, the Spirit filled Glen's life with love for his family, for God's people, and for His Word. I can see Glen now coming to the 6 A.M. Friday men's breakfast at Spears with his precious Bible in hand, eager to soak up some more of its teaching. And Christ gave him a longing to see men and women come home to the Father.

During this time Glen was named chairman of the evangelism committee and we began making calls together. Almost every Tuesday night we would strike out together, often sharing a bit of our lives with each other as we drove to our appointment, then pause for a moment, lifting up a prayer for guidance and openness before we entered a house or an apartment. These were tender, rich times! At first Glen was a bit shy, and would hold back, but then little by little he entered into the conversation. What a joy it was to hear him speak of his coming alive in Christ in his sixties. That was usually the best part of our visit. Now and then we would praise God the following Sunday when someone we had visited would step forward taking their stand for Christ.

How well I recall the night we visited Dan and Pat Black who had worshiped with us for the first time the previous Sunday. They were waiting for us. Dan was a county fireman and Pat a secretary in an insurance office. They quickly came to the point. "We've been married for five months and we want to pray together, but we don't know how. Maybe you could help us." Talk about an open door! When Glen asked if they knew Jesus Christ, the One who really teaches us how to pray, their candor almost took our breath away. "No, but we want to get to know Him, because we hope to make this a

Christian marriage." So there were those precious, hushed moments when they gave themselves to Christ. Their baptism was a glorious event, and later they asked that their marriage be blessed in worship, because they had spoken their vows earlier before a civil judge. This we did one Sunday morning at the conclusion of the service.

And Glen went from strength to strength, not only in calling with the pastor, but in encouraging others to reach out for Christ, in sharing the Gospel with business associates, even speaking to his boss about the Lord. He eventually went "beyond Jerusalem" to share the meaning of Christ in his life out in Judea and Samaria on lay witness teams. As this faithful man became more and more an unashamed witness for Christ, his quiet enthusiasm was a blessing to our entire congregation.

Glen and Alice Holman had a deepening longing to live their lives for the glory of God at home and in the marketplace. When Glen retired from selling coffee, the two of them opened a Dairy Queen restaurant in a small neighboring town and conducted business in a deliberately pastoral way, for both employees and customers. As Glen put it, "We want people to leave having enjoyed themselves because there's 'something different' about our place."

When they opened a newly remodeled building for an expanded business, they asked that it be dedicated to the glory of God. So on a Sunday afternoon, in the midst of their customers, everything paused for songs and Scripture, a statement of commitment and prayer. Not for business reasons, but because the Scripture admonishes us, "So, whether you eat or drink, or whatever you do, do all to the glory of God" (1 Corinthians 10:31).

Then the day came when Glen admitted he was feeling dizzy and confused, having increasing difficulty making sense out of anything he read, even portions of Scripture. After many tests the worst fears were confirmed. This was not migraine headaches, but a large cancerous brain tumor. After surgery, when as much of the malignancy was removed as possible, the surgeon simply informed the family that Glen's days were limited. But how faithfully and even joyously Glen witnessed to God's redeeming grace in those remaining months.

Glen wanted to be in his home for his final days on earth. A wondrous peace filled the house as his family gathered round and ministered day after day. And the friends from hospice were a source of great strength, as was Roy Lassen, a friend and fellow member of long standing. Then one day the call came, and Glen quietly entered the Father's house.

His homegoing service was a mighty celebration of the resurrection. A host of people entered into the singing of joyous choruses and hymns of assurance which Glen had come to love. The "peace that passes understanding" shone on the faces of his beloved family. And all of us praised God when Dan Black, who had gotten permission to be away from his post for a couple of hours, came in uniform to bear witness to the saving power of Jesus Christ, which he had come to know through the witness of Glen Holman. He and his wife, Pat, now had a "real Christian thing going!"

So the invitation was being heard. And people were responding—particularly younger couples, drawn by the Spirit to cast their lot with this great, old downtown church. Coming to join the faithful remnant who had hung on waiting for this day, coming to a party knowing that Jesus would be there.

What a joy it was for Ruth and me to initiate three younger married classes during an eight or nine year period. Lamplighters, Genesis, and Koinonia these classes chose to call themselves. And, of course, that meant babies. Sixty-five or seventy of them in three lovely, freshened-up nurseries where once there had been one or two. Cooing and crying, laughing and playing—a growing chorus of wonderful baby sounds echoing through the halls every Sunday morning, cared for by a dedicated crew of volunteer nursery workers. Here was the promise of the future, that the Lord was gathering His whole family for His final party.

Will You Extend the Invitation?

A living church is an inviting church. But sadly we often become too cozy and ingrown, too "clubby" for people to feel welcome. And we can get so busy promoting all kinds of good programs that we miss the seeking people right under our noses. Or we expect the invitation to be extended by the pastor and a handful of people who make up the evangelism committee. We say that is their specialty or interest, assuming that takes care of it. After all, that's not our kind of thing, we say. But deep down we know this is a copout, a rationalization to cover up our fear or spiritual apathy.

But a healthy body of believers is always a reproducing family. This means that every member — all who have met Christ and received His gift of forgiveness and new life — is a witness. This is not an option, but a way of life. This is good news — like being set free from a death camp or having word that our terribly sick baby is going to make it — and we cannot keep it in. Sooner or later it "leaks out"! We are motivated by Christ's love which has flooded our lives, not by guilt or fear or pressure.

Perhaps your greatest need is to confess that a carelessness, a coldness of heart, an inner barrenness, has robbed you of speaking any word for Christ. And then to pray passionately that Christ would restore in you that first love for Him. For He asks only one question of you, "Simon, son of John, do you love Me more than these?" Your answer will determine whether or not you are His witness.

We will then begin to see people where they are, and leave our "comfort zones" to meet them on their turf. Jesus was doing that all the time — at a well with a guilty woman, in the home of a curious tax collector, finally on a cross welcoming a repentant thief. He is our teacher and model. Where are your friends who have never met Christ? Would you join them there? In a kitchen over a cup of coffee, at a P.T.A. meeting, during a lunch break at the plant, in the clubhouse after a round of golf? Here your friends feel at ease.

And who are these friends to whom you are drawn? These

people who are in your social network? A neighbor, a tennis partner, the man in the labor union you visit with, the girl on your basketball squad, a brother or an aunt? Is this a trusting relationship, deep enough so you don't have to play games with that person, keeping him or her at arm's length, but can talk freely about things that really matter? Do you care deeply enough about that person to pray for him or her daily?

Perhaps you could initiate a house party or a friendship event to which you could bring your friend. Here that person could taste a bit of the life in the body of Christ. In all this there may come a moment—an opening that you may never have again—when you will name Christ's name, tenderly and unashamedly tell that friend the story of His love, and then extend the invitation!

Let a few trusted fellow believers know what you are up to—including your pastor. Ask them to join you in prayer in this new venture. We all need to be accountable.

What would happen in your church if others joined you and an invitation movement got started? Your whole church family could become a party at Matthew's house.

C h a p t e r F i v e

Set Free To Love

*"Her sins, which are many, are forgiven,
for she loved much." Luke 7:47*

Here is a story of reconciliation, the Spirit's gift to the church in Wichita after years of being alienated from a host of former members, now organized as Metropolitan Baptist. The bad news of that severed congregation cannot be avoided. The joy of meeting again as brothers and sisters comes after the anger and bitterness of division. We come to the glory of the Resurrection only after passing through the pain of Black Friday.

There is no way this story can be told in fairness to everyone. Those most deeply involved in this church struggle, even after all these years, have their own versions of this unhappy chapter. I have only attempted to sketch a bit of the bad news to highlight the joy of the good news. My version is not submitted in anger or vindictiveness but in sorrow, and also in gratitude because at the end we knew the healing grace of our Lord. I tell it in the hope that other churches will be encouraged to accept the ministry of reconciliation.

We came to Wichita under no illusions—so we thought. The church had been ruptured and we were coming to serve that faithful group who had somehow managed to hang on to the building through it all. The people had been quite honest with us about the old troubles. And I knew something of the story—after all it had been national news. And I remember wondering at that time, "How could these people get into such a state of affairs?" But that was from a distance!

Now it was different. I was their pastor, one of them. And I began to discover there was more pain and disappointment after fifteen years than I had expected. From time to time it would leak out in some conversation. "Oh, she was one of my best friends, but I haven't seen her for a long time. She joined the 'other church.'" "I don't understand how some of those strong, committed people could have left us to end up in Metropolitan Baptist." And sometimes that leftover, unhealed hostility seemed to color the way people judged others or came to church business meetings expecting that some kind of wrangle would be inevitable.

And I was surprised when I discovered how the aftereffects of that turmoil still lingered in the community. At the first Rotary Club meeting I attended, a longtime attorney, Verne Laing, approached me. "So you're the new pastor at First Baptist Church. Well, my law firm represented your people in that church split, and I am glad that the Kansas Supreme Court finally decided in your church's favor." Quite an introduction.

Some weeks later at a Saturday morning coffee, Joe Kennedy, a partner in Laing's law office, brought up the subject again, with a sly bit of humor. "I probably know more about the ins and outs of First Baptist than most of the members. When that whole thing came up I was just out of law school, new in the firm, and was assigned all the leg work in getting ready to bring the case to court. I ended up reading the minutes of all the business meetings and official reports going back to the church's beginning. Why, I even know who got disciplined over the years and for what reason. Some of that made pretty interesting reading!"

When I reached out for some kind of fellowship of ministers, I found none, except when a few of the downtown pastors met some weeks before Thanksgiving to plan the union service. It seemed the churches were going off in different directions, oblivious to the needs and hopes of sister congregations. In fact, I was so lonely in those first few months I sought out some ministerial colleagues to introduce myself. I missed the warm, trusting relationship I had known with many of my brothers in Sioux Falls. And I wondered if the dissension in First Baptist had not been the sad seed sown which was now being harvested in the "separateness" among these Wichita churches.

But it was the old, yellowed newspaper clippings a friend shared with me that jolted me most—painful stuff that I read with some reluctance. I knew then how deeply involved an entire community had become in this church's troubles. That was plainly evident in the letters that had been written to the editor, some hurting and defensive, others even moralistic, coming from all manner of people, both in and out of the church, stretching out over 1960 and 1961. And the daily headlines were a blow by blow description of the angry struggle for a curious public. "First Baptist Fights On." "Baptist Hassle Taken to Court." "District Court Hears High Baptist Official." And there was one that read "ABC'ers Find Church Locked" over a picture of fifty or so people attempting to conduct their midweek prayer service in the alley next to the church. But the saddest report of all was in the August 3, 1960 issue of the paper. "A suit was filed by a number of church members with the plaintiffs claiming an irreconcilable conflict exists between two factions in the congregation and that these two groups can no longer live in peace and harmony."

No wonder "the First Baptist troubles" became the topic of coffee break conversation with townspeople often taking sides. The skeptics and critics made a joke of the whole thing, relieved they were not a part of any institutional church. Leaders in the religious community found themselves in a quandary, wondering if there were any way they could help. John Hoon, pastor of neighboring St. Paul's Methodist Church, wrote on February 26, 1960, "The situation in our community with reference to our First Baptist friends is something that makes my heart very heavy."

But the deepest embarrassment and pain was within the congregation itself. How do people who bear the name of Christ, and by that very confession claim to be "members of one another," come to the place where there are now "two factions . . . insisting they can no longer live in peace and harmony"? Who sows the seeds of misunderstanding and suspicion which eventually erupt in angry accusations, so that longtime friends no longer speak to one another, business meetings become shouting matches, and hostility bordering on physical violence threatens to break out in the place set aside for prayer? And all this finally brings a congregation to the public courts to settle God's business.

At the bottom every alienation is the work of the evil one who delights in spreading confusion and setting people at odds. Did not the Lord God say, "I will put enmity between you and the woman" (Genesis 3:15) after the serpent had prompted that first act of disobedience in the garden? The friendly hospitality of that place was now poisoned by hostility and separation, infecting all created existence. Disorder crept into the family, the neighborhood, and eventually the affairs of nations. The story of Cain killing his brother Abel and the confusion at the Tower of Babel bear witness to this poison in the human family. Every broken home, every refugee camp, every teenage gang war, and the feverish production of nuclear weapons is a tragic, contemporary testimony to this personal, but cosmic, alienation. *But so is every divided, broken church!*

No wonder Jesus repeatedly unmasked the divisive work of the devil when He confronted His enemies. "He was a murderer from the beginning, and has nothing to do with the truth, because there is no truth in him" (John 8:44). There is the real source of all our division.

So there is the dark, often hidden, side to the story of every church struggle, however much the rightness of any side may be rationalized. There are those strange twists and turns, those circumstances and personalities through which the adversary seeks to weave his evil plot, always attempting to thwart and destroy the work of Christ. Suspicions and accusations infect good people involved in "righteous causes." Who knows what hidden motives, what fear and prejudices, were stimulated and played on by the evil one as he stirred up misunderstanding and division in the Wichita church?

Here was a congregation deeply rooted in the life of American Baptists—the "northern" variety—more open and inclusive than most Baptist groups. A church was born in this wide open cow town named Wichita after an Indian plains tribe, meeting to organize as a congregation in May of 1872 when "twenty-five brave souls gathered in a little store on Main Street." They were sustained in those early years through the prayerful support of "like-minded Baptists" in the East, who also shared what meager financial help they could. It was an appropriate place for Baptists to make their witness here at the confluence of the Arkansas and Little Arkansas Rivers. The specific spiritual and material ties with "those Baptists in the East" were crucial in the court case which was to come ninety years later.

Over the years this church became a mighty force for Christ. Some of its well-known members were leading decision-makers in the community, believing the Gospel should make a difference in the marketplace. And the church was not ashamed to advertise its commitment by hanging a great cross-shaped sign on the corner of the building lighted with the words "Famous for the Gospel."

These people did not play a game of isolation, but enthusiastically joined with other Christians to form the Wichita Council of Churches, which developed a nationally recognized public school released-time religious education program. And they eagerly supported the mission program of the American Baptists, even hosting the national convention in 1941.

Then in 1945 a gifted evangelist pulpiteer from Texas came to be pastor of this church. W.C. Coleman, whose opinion was never taken lightly, was convinced after hearing him preach that he was "the right man to lead our church." After some persuasion this man agreed to come, giving assurance he would never sever the ties of the church with its parent denomination. Apparently there seemed to be some need for such a promise, because he had such strong emotional ties "deep in the heart of Texas."

As people streamed into Wichita from the south in those years, particularly Oklahoma and Texas, to work in the aircraft plants, hundreds of them joined First Baptist. They knew little about the roots and historic commitments of the church they were joining. They were drawn to it by the warm, anecdotal, envangelistic preaching of the pastor. Church membership peaked at 4,300 in those days and Sunday School attendance often topped 2,000. George Hilton, "the Baptist barber," a fine amateur photographer, told of climbing up a ladder in a morning service to get a picture of the one-thousandth baptism during this pastor's ministry from "just the right angle."

Little by little the direction and style of the church's ministry changed. A particular kind of pulpit-centered evangelistic sermon and invitation became almost the exclusive diet in worship. More and more of the Sunday School classes began using Southern Baptist literature and it was architects from the Southern Baptist Sunday School Board who planned the new five-story educational building. The deacons no longer took Communion to shut-ins, for that was "unbaptistic" and smacked of Rome. Many church decisions, such as major building programs and budget matters and calling of staff, were made by a small, select group, who then passed them on to the Board of Deacons and the congregation for formal approval if necessary.

Through all this the people who had strong American Baptist ties felt more and more excluded. "What is happening to this church?" they wondered. "Where are we headed?"

Then in 1957 W.C. Coleman, widely respected as a wise, godly leader and a restraining influence in the congregation, died. His going left a great gap in the ranks and further weakened the ties of the church with its parent denomination over which he had presided as president in 1928.

The final, vexing issue in the growing confusion within the church became the relationship of the American Baptist Convention to the National Council of Churches. American Baptists had been charter members of this cooperative fellowship of Protestant and Orthodox churches and took this commitment very seriously.

But the National Council would frequently come under angry attack whenever its General Board sought to make prophetic statements on peace and race, housing and poverty, seeking to be a voice for the poor and disenfranchised. To compound matters, about this time the Air Force issued a widely read pamphlet accusing the National Council of being infiltrated by communists and left-wingers. This caused even more consternation among those leading First Baptist at the time and deepened the suspicion that American Baptists had really bedded down with the enemy. Eventually it was made clear that the pamphlet was the work of hatemongers, much of it based on distortions and falsehoods. After considerable protest it was finally withdrawn, but the damage had already been done.

All the suspicions now seemed confirmed for those who mistrusted the Convention. Was not First Baptist weakening its witness and being led astray through its denominational affiliation? Yoked with questionable, even unholy allies? In the face of these charges, a minority struggled to explain and defend the relationship of the church with the American Baptist Convention. After all, they knew many of the denominational leaders to be people of spiritual integrity, and were aware how the Lord had blessed the ABC mission program through amazing growth and outreach.

But the ones who were now leading the church felt it was imperative to investigate these charges. So a handpicked committee of ten was appointed to "check out the facts." A perfunctory action, it seemed, for it was almost a foregone conclusion there would be a proposal to withdraw all financial support for the American Baptist Convention.

In the midst of this growing uncertainty and turmoil, key denominational leaders made special attempts at reconciling the differences, urging the people to consider the direction the church was taking and to look at other options. Both William Keucher, the executive secretary of the Kansas Baptist Convention, and Edwin Tuller, the general secretary of the American Baptist Convention—wise, irenic men with a passion for the unity of Christ's body—came as peacemakers. They sought to make it clear that the congregation could decide that none of the missionary money given to the American Baptist Convention would go to the National Council. But the deeper issue, they both felt, was the serious negative repercussions any divisive action would have on the cause of Christ.

But it was to no avail. Those in leadership had already decided the course the church should take.

Now began a series of sad decisions which finally led to the rupture of the church. On March 4, 1960, the church heard the report of the Committee of Ten and voted to withdraw all financial support from the American Baptist Convention and any of its affiliated organizations. The vote was 1,170 to 235.

On March 16, 1960, a letter was sent by the education department of the church to all officers and teachers advising them to be in accord with the resolution of March 9, or tender their resignation. This forced many loyal ABC workers who had voted against the resolution into a very difficult position.

At a July 13, 1960 meeting of the congregation a resolution to discontinue affiliation with the ABC and related organizations was adopted. The vote was 739 to 294.

The minority group now began to worship in the chapel, attempting to maintain their integrity as an American Baptist church. This caused the majority to insist that any meetings in the building must be in the sanctuary at the regularly scheduled times. Consequently, when the American Baptist group insisted on meeting in the chapel, they were locked out and finally forced to worship elsewhere for many months.

The question had now become identity and ownership! Which group had the right to claim the real estate at Second and Broadway as their spiritual home? There was no way two groups "who could no longer live in peace and harmony" were willing to settle the matter among themselves. So the issue was brought to district court by the American Baptist minority group. Here before a courtroom crowded with both the concerned and the curious each group argued its case, claiming it was rightfully "their building." The American Baptists lost. The judge ruled in favor of the majority.

So the decision was appealed and the case was finally heard before the Kansas Supreme Court, which reversed the verdict of the lower court by a unanimous decision, giving possession of the building to the much smaller group. This ruling, made public on May 5, 1962, concluded that the "denomination of a Baptist church cannot be changed by a mere majority vote." The group most closely identified in purpose and affiliation with the original founders was entitled to the building.

The final human judgment had been made, it seemed. The chasm now separating this split family had become too deep to bridge. So each part of the broken body went its own way — separated, carrying the embarrassment and wounds of the division.

The smaller group, which had dwindled to "180 regular members, sixty percent of them active," according to one report, now returned to claim the building at Second and Broadway, to unlock all those rooms, most of which would not be used for years. However, they first had to untangle a confusing mess of keys which had been left in anger by the other group. This was really a symbol of the spiritual shambles into which the church had fallen. The much larger group — well over 1,000 — now began meeting in Southeast High School while their new church home was being built across the river.

But the sad story had not yet come to its last chapter. For

when the larger group officially affiliated with the Southern Baptist Convention as Metropolitan Baptist Church, those who did not want to be a part of any convention withdrew to form Beth-Eden Baptist Church, an independent congregation. Division usually breeds fragmentation. One cannot help but grieve over the drain of spiritual and emotional and financial resources during those sad years, and the lost opportunities for witness and service which would never be regained, but most of all over the scandal of Christ's body being torn asunder.

But how easy to cast stones in all this, to sit in judgment, to self-righteously insist this would never have happened had I been around. But to do so is to assume that I am without sin, to forget about my own hidden, unhealed angers and jealousies which can break forth at the most unexpected times. A petulant, "I'll get you people straightened out" kind of sermon, or a self-centered outburst in a diaconate meeting, or turning aside from someone who has disagreed with *my* program—any of these can tear down rather than build up, exclude instead of include, destroy relationships instead of drawing people together. Perhaps the "Wichita story" is more my story than I realize.

What happens when someone moves in on the turf I protect so jealously? *My* books, or *my* reserved parking place, or even *my* schedule or *my* pulpit or *my* status in the community? Within a congregation, that turf can be the keys to the kitchen or the organ or even a Sunday School class. How much we are like those ten disciples who became angry when they discovered James and John, with the help of their mother, had petitioned Jesus for the best seats in His kingdom!

Why do I become so disturbed when the pastor down the street reports great crowds with all kinds of people responding to the invitation? And have you ever heard anyone in the church ask in a self-pitying tone, "Why don't I get asked to sing solos anymore? I can sing much better than a lot of those younger ones who get called on all the time," or "How did Joe White get elected a deacon? I've been a member much longer than he has, and did anyone bother to check on his family life before they asked him?" Was it not that kind of jealousy that drove Cain to kill Abel?

Or I can become a self-appointed defender of the truth and refuse to hear any other point of view. The spirit of Pharisaism dies hard in all of us. Or I can dogmatically insist that people must have "my kind of spiritual experience." The spiritual superiority of those tongues-speaking Christians in Corinth is with us to this day. Or I can push a legalistic lifestyle, insisting that certain "do's" and "don'ts" are a necessary part of salvation. Little wonder that Paul had to speak in such strong words to those Galatian Christians who were giving up their liberty in Christ, falling back into the old ways of "circumcision salvation."

And the list goes on! How critical I can become of someone who disagrees with me, failing to understand this brother or sister who has clay feet just as I do. Or I may have a subtle spirit of prejudice, feeling at ease with those who are poor or black, but quietly hardening my heart toward the ones who are rich in the things of this world but seem unconcerned about the dispossessed. Or I may take a condescending attitude toward those who appear to belong to the self-righteous "in" crowd, the "professional" Bible students.

When this kind of negative, destructive spirit is let loose in the church, it can wound and divide the body. It is so easy for us to condemn those fleshly sins, "immorality, impurity, licentiousness," when Paul lists the "works of the flesh," and conveniently pass over "enmity, strife . . . anger . . . dissension, and a party spirit," which are also on the list. We can forget that the apostle goes on to say, "Those who do such things shall not inherit the kingdom of God" (Galatians 5:19-21).

I do not have to look far for illustrative material. It is right at hand. This is being written on the porch of our small cottage on Lobster Lake in Minnesota, a place full of family memories, built in the thirties by my father and his brother on a strip of property belonging to the "clan." But now the cottage down the hill to the north has been sold by my cousin to outsiders, people who do not know the habits and free ways of our family. So when our grandchildren innocently started crossing their property on their way for a swim, which they had always done before, they were suddenly stopped by the new owner. "This no longer belongs to your family, so don't come on our property anymore."

Now I had angry, defensive feelings and engaged in some careless talk about our neighbors. The next day an opportunity to get even came when one of their daughters crossed our property. Just as I was about to shout, "This is our property. You're not to cross it," "something," or Someone, closed my mouth and choked back the words. For me a small miracle!

Then an unexpected impulse came to me. An alternative which at first I resisted. "Why not pray for these neighbors?" "But I hardly know them." "And you are trying to write about being set free to love." How could I answer that? So I gave in and reluctantly breathed a rather feeble prayer for these "strangers," and for myself, that I might understand and accept them. I was grateful afterward that the Spirit had sparked me into uttering even that simple petition.

And the answer came far more quickly than I could have ever imagined. For the next afternoon during a family gathering, just as we were having the cake celebrating my mother's ninety-third birthday, we noticed frantic excitement at this neighbor's place, people running in all directions trying to extinguish a rubbish fire which had gotten out of hand and was spreading rapidly over a dead, grassy area on this extremely dry, hot day. Many of our group, including this "reluctant servant," responded immediately, and went running with shovels and a rake and even a hose, almost as if we were a trained volunteer fire department. In a few minutes the fire was extinguished.

As these neighbors were expressing thanks, I was surprised at the words I found myself uttering. Did not our Lord say there would be occasions when the Holy Spirit would give us the words? I am certain that is so even in these lowly kinds of circumstances. "This whole bunch of relatives is celebrating my mother's ninety-third birthday today. That's why we're all here. Why don't you come up and join us for some cake and a cold drink or coffee?" Which they did! And we found ourselves getting to know these folks over birthday cake. It turned out to be more of a celebration than I had counted on. Now these people are our friends, and have even volunteered to help us clean fish.

How different it would have been had I allowed my defensive anger to take over! But there is another way. "If we live by the Spirit, let us also walk by the Spirit" (Galatians 5:25).

So as the months passed, I found myself brooding over the "church situation" in Wichita, more and more dissatisfied with the status quo. Surely this was unfinished business. It was obvious these two churches—First and Metropolitan—would continue having their distinct identities and missions. But were we always going to live separated by a wall—carrying bad memories and unresolved angers, or at best simply ignoring one another? Was there not some better way than that? Was not Christ praying that we might discover again our oneness in Him, and know that we were fellow citizens in His household? And what about His new commandment that we are to love one another even as He has loved us? Was not this the clearest evidence that all men would know we are His disciples? Were these only nice Christian words we throw around, or were we willing to take them seriously enough to obey Him? If we did, would we not move toward one another? Had not Christ broken down all the old barriers through His shed blood and opened the way?

I recall the day I "crossed the river" and cautiously walked into the Metropolitan church building, a great brick edifice with its clean-cut spire piercing the sky. I remember standing hushed in the dimly lighted sanctuary with its impressive marble pulpit and red opera chairs, wondering, was this "enemy" or "friendly" territory? And also asking, "Lord, what do You have in store for us?" Later I was to discover this was hospitable ground when I visited with the interim pastor in his study and we parted with prayer. Healing—physical, spiritual, and emotional—always begins quietly and unnoticed.

And there is special timing in God's doings. I was surprised some time later when Preston Huston, a layman from Metropolitan Baptist Church who had been so deeply involved in the struggle, called me one Sunday asking if he could bring a friend by my office that afternoon. Of course I was delighted. I had come to know Preston casually through Rotary, and since he managed his own ad agency, he had agreed to serve as publicity chairman for the upcoming Leighton Ford Reachout. Now he was eager that this "friend," who was considering becoming their pastor, and I should meet each other. When they entered the office, I could easily understand that this tall, friendly, athletic-appearing man had played football at Arkansas under Frank Broyles, and then stayed on for a couple of years as one of the assistant coaches before going to seminary. Pres explained that I was general chairman of the Leighton Ford Reachout, and should Phil come as their pastor he was hopeful their church would really "get into" this evangelistic effort. That simple act of their coming over on "our turf" had quietly opened another door. I rejoiced when it was later announced that Phil Lineberger had accepted the call of Metropolitan Baptist.

Phil had not been on the scene too long when I was asked if I would be willing to share my vocational classification with him so that he might become a member of the Rotary Club. A small favor indeed. The day Pres Huston introduced him as a new member, he indicated, "Roger Fredrikson has shared his vocational classification with our new pastor." Then he went on to say, "You know, there is a new spirit between First Baptist and Metropolitan." And there was spontaneous applause, which says something about what people expect of the church. I was out of town and missed this moment, but a Presbyterian friend called that evening to give me the report.

Then in the fall of 1980 Leighton Ford came to town for an evangelistic Reachout. We had prayed and planned and worked, preparing for this event for almost two years, grateful that this thoughtful, creative evangelist was eager to lead us in our dreams and hopes to penetrate the community for Christ. Before it was over, more than 150 churches had joined together in this cause—a minor miracle, because the religious community was so splintered. We literally had to reach out and find spiritual allies, even convince reluctant pastors that they would not compromise their convictions by joining with other evangelical Christians.

How could we best prepare? We had no structure, no single ministerial fellowship or church council as a rallying point. Would we be able to call the believing community together and kindle in every church a new passion to reach out for Christ? We could only try—with the Spirit's help. And this we set out to do.

Eighty of us pastors spent a day with George Hunter who helped us understand how every congregation could become a contagious center of life. Nearly 3,000 people were equipped in Christian life and witness classes to counsel those who might respond to the call of Christ. Scores of homes were opened as all kinds of people gathered to help one another become "lovers for Christ." Much to our surprise hundreds of men showed up at the Beech Activity Center in spite of a blinding snowstorm to hear Leighton call them to become bold spokesmen for Christ.

Glen Holman surprised us all that night when he stood up to spontaneously share the new joy in his life because he had obeyed the impulse of the Spirit to speak to a fellow businessman about Christ. This friend was with him. Glen's words underlined everything Leighton had urged us to undertake.

The city was honeycombed with small prayer groups meeting in homes and offices and restaurants. A week before the Reachout, neighbors gathered in several hundred homes for a social time to watch a TV special on Channel 3. Here Leighton dealt with Christ's deepest answers to our loneliness, our guilt, and our search for meaning. It was a bold attempt to touch our community for Christ!

Finally September 21 came! That first night was a wondrous experience, long to be remembered—the fervent, hopeful time of prayer before the service, the beautiful sound of God's family greeting one another as they came together, the air of expectancy which filled the Convention Hall of Century II as we walked to the platform! Then there was the strong, vibrant music and the compelling call Leighton issued in behalf of Christ, and those first brave souls coming nervously but obediently, responding to the promptings of the Spirit!

And so it went for eight nights—celebrations of hope and renewal. During those days Christians came to know and love one another and the fresh winds of the Spirit blew through old, tired churches and sinners came to discover the grace and forgiveness of our Saviour. Wichita had not experienced such a joyful family festival in decades.

I was delighted when my eighty-six-year-old mother, who sang in the choir every night, was introduced on youth night as the "youngest" person there. Is there ever a time when we retire from serving the Lord?

And through it all many of the people from First Baptist and Metropolitan Baptist were moving toward one another. They could not stand next to each other in the choir lifting up songs of salvation or meet at the front while counseling those making decisions without the Lord stirring up something new. If we could meet as friends in Century II, why not in one of our sanctuaries?

So one day over coffee—what else?—Phil Lineberger and I had an open, candid visit about all this. Was it possible the Lord had allowed us to have this Reachout so that our people might be brought together again? Both of us were of a common mind. Our churches would never be completely free to minister in the Spirit until we had come together in an act of worship and fellowship, letting go of the old and moving into God's new day as brothers and sisters in Christ's family. So we convenanted that day we would open up this possibility with our church leaders. I expressed the hope that in God's good time First Baptist might invite Metropolitan to join with us in some kind of "special worship service." So we parted, prayerfully and hopefully.

I came with some trembling and wonder to our next board meeting, knowing I must open my heart to these dear people. This was a moment of decision and opportunity, when a pastor must lead or be unfaithful to his calling. And I knew in my deepest heart, although I never voiced it openly to anyone except my wife, that I had come to a point of no return. My ministry in this place was at stake. I simply would not have the will to stay on among these people if they turned aside from this moment of opportunity.

The possibility of inviting the Metropolitan people to join with us in worship was not a political or public relations matter. It was an urgent spiritual matter, an issue deeper than deciding on the size of the budget or tackling another new program or renovating some part of the building. We would never be renewed until we had reached out to greet and worship with those from whom we had been separated. Had this not already begun to happen as we had sung and prayed and counseled with people from Metropolitan during the Leighton Ford Reachout?

But most compelling of all was the word of Scripture. Every Sunday we prayed, "Forgive us our debts as we forgive our debtors." And had not Jesus said, "If you are offering your gift at the altar, and there remember that your brother has something against you, leave your gift there before the altar and go; first be reconciled to your brother, and then come and offer your gift" (Matthew 5:23-24). And what about that awesome statement in Ephesians, "For He is our peace, who has made us both one, and has broken down the dividing wall of hostility" (Ephesians 2:14). What did all this have to say to us about our relationship to Metropolitan Baptist? Had not the time come for us to move toward one another in some kind of healing gesture?

This was the hope I expressed. There was a long, hushed moment as I waited for some kind of response. Then a newer member spoke up. "I believe our pastor is right. This is what the Lord expects us to do. Such a move is long overdue." Others voiced the same opinion. But some of our older members, those who had been through the struggle, voiced their honest misgivings. "Why open up all that again?" "Why not let sleeping dogs lie?" But had not our Lord refused to let "sleeping dogs" lie when He dealt with all our guilt and alienation at the cross?

There was further discussion. "If we invited Metropolitan to worship with us, would they accept?" "We would have to risk that. Their pastor is discussing this possibility with their deacons." "When would we have such a service?" "Probably on a Sunday evening. That can be worked out if Metropolitan accepts our invitation." "Would we then join with them for a worship experience in their church later?" "Yes, that is our hope."

The meeting concluded with an extraordinary session of prayer when men and women earnestly sought to know the mind and will of Christ. We left agreeing we would make a final decision on the matter a month later at our next meeting.

In the meantime there was considerable conversation throughout our church family, much of it positive and hopeful, a bit of it fearful and negative. Many older members, who had been deeply hurt, came speaking quiet words of encouragement. "This is something we need to do." At the next board meeting the group had a common mind to go ahead. I praise God for those courageous people who obeyed the wooing of the Spirit and voted to extend the invitation. So a letter of invitation dated December 22, 1980, was sent to Metropolitan. It read in part:

Dr. Phil Lineberger
and Members of Metropolitan Baptist Church

Greetings in the name of Christ
from the people of First Baptist!

After discussion and prayer we invite you to share in our evening service on February 22. We would want to have Pastor Lineberger give the evening message and your choir or some other music group to lead us in the ministry of music. We believe that this can be a time of worship and celebration to the glory of God.

Following the service we invite you to stay for a time of coffee and fellowship.

For some years now our scriptural theme has been, "Behold, I am making all things new." And we believe that the Lord of the church is renewing all of us. It is in this spirit of a new day for both our churches that we extend this invitation.

In the bonds of the Spirit,

The letter was signed by Douglas Johnson, chairman of the Board; Fred Loseke, the church moderator; and the pastor.

Meanwhile over at Metropolitan the deacons were struggling to come to a decision. Their pastor had been there a relatively short time and some of them wondered what he was trying to get them into. And some insisted at the outset, "Why should we go over there when those people stole the building from us?" But there was also a strong group who believed that the time had come for us to meet together. It was their chairman, Preston Huston, who carried the day. He believed that this was the right thing to do and openly stated, "I want to see this happen while I am chairman of the board." So after a couple of meetings their board voted to accept our invitation.

When I learned of this, I asked Preston if he would read their letter of acceptance in person in our morning worship service. After a moment of hesitation he quietly answered, "Yes, I think I can do that." When he entered our sanctuary that Communion Sunday to share their response, an audible buzz of anticipation ran through the congregation. The paper trembled, but the voice was strong as he read the words.

Dr. Roger Fredrikson
and members of First Baptist Church

Greetings from the people of
Metropolitan Baptist Church!

We heartily accept your invitation to lead in a worship service at First Baptist Church on February 22, 1981. We plan to bring our sanctuary choir to help in worship.

We want to invite you to come and lead us in worship on Sunday, March 8, 1981, for the evening service. We want Dr. Fredrikson to preach and the First Baptist choir to lead in worship and celebration. We also want you to stay for a time of fellowship afterward.

There is a sense of great excitement and expectancy concerning these times of worship. We sense a great revival as a result of our getting together again.

Sincerely your friend,

It was signed by the pastor, Phil Lineberger, and the chairman of the board of deacons.

No sooner had he finished when a shout rang out and spontaneous, joyous applause filled the sanctuary. A promise of things to come.

On the Friday preceding that first service, some of us gathered for prayer in the pastor's study at Metropolitan Baptist. I rejoiced that Hal and Zattie Moody from our church, devoted American Baptists who had been through so much of the hurt in earlier years, were willing to join us—in spite of their misgivings. And also that we were able to keep the newspaper reporter, who had somehow learned of the meeting, from making a public event of our sacred time together.

Then that unforgettable night came—Sunday, February 22, 1981. The service was to begin at seven, but people began arriving shortly after six. The folks from Metropolitan seemed eager to walk again on familiar ground and our people didn't want to miss a thing. They knew they were coming to a party. One could feel it in the air. The 900 orders of worship were distributed long before the service began and still the people kept coming. What a wonderful predicament. The eagerness of the people to celebrate the faithfulness of God outran our limited expectations.

Those of us who were to lead the service had gathered in the pastor's study to pray. A holy time of anticipation and empowering! Just as we were about to begin Sheldon Coleman, the son of W.C., now the chief executive officer of the Coleman Company and a member of Metropolitan Baptist, came bounding up the stairs into the study like an excited junior higher. "I'm so glad we're doing this. It should have happened long ago." Later he was quoted in the *Eagle-Beacon:* "Look at it—you can feel it. There's nothing here but fellowship. The past is past. I think it's a wonderful thing. Marvelous."

The whole service of praise and thanks was a joyful overflow of the Spirit, like something being let loose that had been bottled up for years. We were blessed by the warm word of greeting from Doug Johnson, who was now our moderator, and the response of Preston Huston, and by the strong message by Phil Lineberger on our inescapable obligation to be disciples, as well as the music by the Metropolitan choir and ensemble. But it was after the congregation had sung with great abandon, "Great Is Thy Faithfulness," and "Blessed Assurance," that we had a special touch of heaven. When people were encouraged to greet one another, they moved from all over the sanctuary with tears and laughter to embrace or clasp the hands of old and new friends. What a holy, joyous confusion. We could sense the risen Christ moving among us with His word of Shalom.

And we were drawn together at the Father's throne as we joined in prayer. First led by Ed Friesen, our Christian Education chairman, who had been through it all, then by Jesse Vardaman of Metropolitan, who had served both churches as associate pastor. When people were invited to join in spontaneously, audible prayer broke out all over the sanctuary—a healing chorus of confession and gratitude like the sound of "many waters." How fitting that we should sing at the conclusion, "When We All Get to Heaven." Some wondered if we hadn't already arrived. And folks simply lingered over coffee and conversation in the fellowship time that followed as if they did not want to part. The social committee had more faith than the rest of us, for the cookies they had prepared did not run out as the orders of worship had!

Two weeks later we journeyed to Metropolitan for another celebration. For most of our people entering that sanctuary was a "first experience." Once again we knew the touch of the Spirit as our choir and ensemble led in song and I preached on "Our First Nickname." "And in Antioch the disciples were for the first time called Christians" (Acts 11:26). As I stood to preach I was deeply moved to notice that some of our people, particularly Glen Johnston and Roy Lassen, who had been most deeply involved in the struggle, were on hand—participating!

And what was taking place among the believers of these two churches did not go unnoticed. It was almost as if that first nickname was once again being discovered. The newspapers and TV people, without solicitation, picked up the news. People I didn't know would stop me at the most unexpected places—in a grocery store or a filling station or on the way to the bank—to ask, "Aren't you the pastor of First Baptist Church? We're certainly happy about what is happening between your churches." I could only thank them and go on praising God. When Christians who have been alienated are reunited in love, that's good news even in the marketplace.

Whenever there is reconciliation, the healing of relationships, a building up in this broken, divided, estranged world, a sign of hope has been introduced! There is an alternative to antagonism and alienation.

How unexpectedly we stumbled into this alternative in the Olevesta Church in Tallinn, Estonia in 1983. For there we experienced the "ripple effect" of our "Wichita healing" in an almost electrifying way. Another of the Spirit's serendipities! Phil Lineberger and I found ourselves on the same team, moving about the Soviet Union on a friendship preaching mission. On a gray, overcast Easter Sunday night, we ended up in Tallinn, a brave city that lived for decades under foreign occupation. We had just flown in from Kiev, where we had an interesting encounter with the KGB and Intourist people.

The Baptists in Tallinn worship in what was formerly a Lutheran cathedral, an imposing building set on a hill that dominates the skyline. I was asked, among others, to bring an Easter greeting in the evening service, which in their culture really means a brief sermon. As I climbed the steps to the high pulpit I could not help noticing the small electric heater placed there to at least keep the feet warm. Then I saw why, for as I looked out over the expectant congregation filling that huge sanctuary, I saw that most of them were bundled in overcoats. Then one of those unexpected urges struck me, "Why not have Phil join you up here?" Hoping this to be the Spirit's prompting, I was relieved when he accepted my sudden invitation.

As we stood there together, I shared briefly the story of our churches coming together to worship after years of alienation. And what a miracle it was that the two of us—pastors of these churches—should be on this team. Then I spoke those strong words of Jesus, "By this all men will know that you are My disciples, if you have love for one another" (John 13:35). For a moment we embraced. As I prayed I could hear what sounded like a sob—a quiet moan—rising up from the congregation.

After the service there was such animated conversation among the members that we wondered what had taken place. Then Ants Rebane, our gracious host, one of the strong pastors of the Olevesta Church, explained. There had been bitter differences in that congregation, even talk of a split. Now these people had seen in that simple word and act in the pulpit what could happen among them. Why could they not move toward one another in love and forgiveness rather than stubbornly resist one another? This they had already begun to do, Ants reported with great joy. The risen Christ was breaking down the barriers and opening the channels of love among them. What a way to celebrate Easter! Who could have imagined that two separated churches in Wichita, Kansas, moving toward one another, might touch and renew a church in Estonia? God's ways are wondrously strange!

As I left that special Easter service in Tallinn, I could not help marveling at what the Lord was doing among us back at Second and Broadway. We were experiencing a new freedom—the freedom to love! We had taken the risk of moving toward fellow Christians from whom we had been separated. And now we were being loosed from old fears and animosities, becoming more open with our Lord and with one another, more eager to welcome the stranger and openly voice a concern for the spiritual and physical welfare of the city.

And that was happening to me as well. I remember sitting at my desk one Monday morning hearing the wail of an ambulance siren. How often I had heard that sound here at this busy downtown intersection, but never as I did that day. I wondered who was being taken to the hospital this time, and then found myself breathing a prayer for whoever it might be. I suddenly realized that I had come to love this city with all its hurts and joys, its needs and possibilities. I was no longer a stranger here. This was *my* city.

But that love, being released among our people, was far more than a sentimental feeling or another program. It was a reality, a gift, which Christ was sharing with us through His mighty reconciling transaction at the cross. "In Christ God was reconciling the world to Himself" (2 Corinthians 5:19). Paul puts it so succinctly but completely, in writing to those proud, troubled Christians in Corinth.

And when we are drawn "into Christ," accepting all He has done for us in His saving act, we become "new creations," forgiven, free now to love, to become a part of His continuing reconciling work. The apostle goes on to say, "All this is from God, who through Christ reconciled us to Himself and gave us the ministry of reconciliation . . . God making His appeal through us" (2 Corinthians 5:18, 20). This is not some starry-eyed, "do good" venture, but a costly, even embarrassing work which we are constrained to undertake. Someone has to make the first move. And there may be rejection, which the One who opened the way for us knew so well. "Father, forgive them; for they know not what they do" (Luke 23:34). So we must return again and again to that holy place of reconciliation, knowing this as the place we live as well as the source of our ministry.

We had caught a fresh glimpse of that reconciling ministry in our experience of meeting with Metropolitan, and not as something to be practiced only at special occasions, but as a way of life, very personal and specific! This calling that cannot be turned on and off depending on who we are dealing with, what day of the week it is, or how we are feeling! If we have died and our life is "hid with Christ in God," then we are to "put on then, as God's chosen ones, holy and beloved, compassion, kindness, lowliness, meekness, and patience, forbearing one another and, if one has a complaint against another, forgiving each other; as the Lord has forgiven you, so you also must forgive. And above all these put on love, which binds everything together in perfect harmony" (Colossians 3:3, 12-14).

This is the Shalom of the Spirit, the Christlike style, the openness and trust which most churches desperately need to "put on." . . . When the pastor loses on a pet project, or doesn't get the salary raise he expected, or learns that the church moderator is critical of him, or his children are being "talked about" because of their behavior. . . . Or when there are tangled feelings and hasty motions being thrown about in a church business meeting. . . . Or when there are hostile differences over redoing the constitution or a building improvement project. . . . Or when the young come in with wild ideas and loud music and the elderly complain that it used to be so quiet around here before "they" came. . . . Or when the strong become impatient with the weak and the slow.

Then are we willing to be "forbearing" and "forgiving"? Who will be the first to move out, to say, "I'm sorry; will you forgive me"? Or admit, "I was wrong. I can see that now. Believe it or not, I'm changing my mind"? Or, "I've avoided you because I really haven't known you. I wonder if we could get together some time and visit"? Tough but healing words.

The alternative is to settle for a kind of ho-hum institution where everyone keeps his safe distance and we play at maintaining church. Or even fall back into being cantankerous and self-centered, insisting on having our own way, filled with the old enmities, "gratifying the desires of the flesh" and being potential church-splitters.

The renewal that must take place in most churches has to do with the healing of relationships, deliverance from a critical spirit and a gossiping tongue, learning again to submit to one another because of reverence for Christ, laughing with those who rejoice and weeping with those who sorrow, truly becoming a place of caring and healing. First Baptist would never have dared welcome and help resettle refugees from Laos and Cambodia and VietNam, never have begun to feed the hungry and clothe the naked, if we had not been set free to love.

I realize now in these later years how much I owe my father, who was a healer, a lover in a great, Christlike way. As a lad of nine I remember asking my mother why Dad was talking so much at night after we had gone to bed. She replied, "Your father is praying." "What is he praying about?" "That God will heal this church that has been so badly split. He is asking the Lord to bring back the people who left in anger some time ago." That caused me to wonder. It was almost a year later when the two "opposing" leaders met one another at the front of the church during the invitation hymn.

What a surprise. Neither knew the other was coming. And as they greeted one another with tears of love and repentance, God's healing work had begun. That was when the revival really got underway! What a look of joy there was on my father's face! Eventually all those who had left were welcomed back into the fellowship.

Fifty-three years later I visited that church, the Sun Prairie Baptist Church, for their centennial celebration. This strong, vibrant country church was having a joyful party praising God for His life among them. And a number of folks made the point of saying, "The Lord used your father to save this church." When we are set free to love, miracles always take place.

Who Makes the First Move?

The most festering hindrance to revival in church after church is broken relationships and old antagonisms that have never been healed. They become like running sores that poison the body of Christ. A heated argument in a Sunday School class, snubbed feelings over someone being overlooked when the church leaders were recognized, the pastor's pet project being rejected, a disagreement over the color of the carpet—it all seemed so minor at the time. But then there were angry feelings and loose talk which clogged the channels of trust and communication. Now a party spirit has divided the people of God and the Spirit is grieved and cannot minister.

Have you ever been involved in such a rupture, literally crippling the body of Christ? I hope not, but if so, how seriously have you taken Jesus' strong words, "If you are offering your gift at the altar, and there remember that your brother [sister] has something against you, leave your gift there before the altar and go; first be reconciled to your brother [sister], and then come and offer your gift" (Matthew 5:23-24). Quite specific, isn't it? And not an option, but a mandate! But the Lord can do a new thing among His people only if they obey that word! Could that mean you are to make the first move toward that one from whom you have been alienated? And you will never go in your own strength — too many fears and arguments will hold you back — but only because Christ has forgiven you at tremendous cost! And has given you His Spirit of power and love and the words of reconciliation for this occasion.

Yes, there can be humiliation and even fear in breaking the silence as you cross the barriers reaching out toward this one from whom you have been separated. Everything in our culture belittles such a move: "Forget it. How stupid can you be?" "It was her fault." "Let her come to you." But who is to have the last word? Our culture or our Lord? Are we not to be transformers rather than conformists? So we go to be reconciled because we have been to the cross and belong to the family of everlasting Shalom.

And you cannot assure yourself in advance that this will be a successful encounter. You might walk into cold defensiveness or a casual brush-off. "Why, there's nothing to talk about." Or, "You know it was your fault." But wonder of wonders, this could be an eternal moment of healing, joy in the morning after the night of separation. Once again the Spirit will be unleashed. What do you suppose might happen in your church now?

Or perhaps Christ is longing to deliver you from a critical spirit and a loose tongue. You have been continually complaining about the inability of others to live up to the standards you have set for them. Jesus said something about that too — seeing the speck of sawdust in your brother's eye while paying no attention to the plank in your own eye. How frequently the Scripture speaks of the danger of a wagging tongue which is like a destructive fire. Are you willing to let the Spirit of Christ fill you with patience and kindness and take control of your tongue? Then your speech will become gentle and constructive — seasoned with salt — and the body will be built up.

Every church needs affirmers, people who are encouragers. "I'm grateful for you." "Thanks for all you've done." "I truly love you in Christ." "I'm praying for you, my sister." Don't you suppose when that spirit begins to pervade a body of believers—not only in worship services, but in board meetings, the church offices, the Sunday School classes, and even in casual settings—renewal may be on the way? The church now becomes a winsome, attractive community drawing the seekers and nonbelievers to the One whose Shalom is filling the people.

Chapter Six

Journey into Compassion

"Is not this the fast that I choose. . . . Is it not to share your bread with the hungry, and bring the homeless poor into your house; when you see the naked, to cover him?" Isaiah 58:6-7

Sitting next to Dean Scholer in a chapel service at Northern Baptist Seminary, I could not help noticing how he rather surreptitiously wiped away a tear now and then. He was listening to a very simple story being told by a plain appearing elderly layman. Part of the impact was the surprise of it all. What could this retired schoolteacher from Wichita, Kansas possibly have to say to a seminary community in Chicago?

Yet here was this crowd of theologues listening carefully to every word this man uttered, caught up in the unpretentious, soft-spoken eloquence of his story. He had started, obviously nervous, shuffling his carefully prepared notes, pausing awkwardly occasionally, for he stuttered. But as he moved along, an excitement welled up in him. Something had happened to him in these later years and he was eager to let us in on it.

I had been asked to give the Browne Lectures on Christian Communication at Northern, and agreed to do so if a couple of our laypeople could join me in telling their story. Perhaps I needed them along for support. Lecturing in seminaries has not exactly been "my thing." Whatever my motive, the seminary accepted the arrangement, perhaps somewhat out of curiosity. How would this pastor and a couple of lay folk get along in a seminary setting?

So I sought out Harold Leffingwell, having the time of his life heading up a ministry of feeding and clothing the hungry and naked, and Kathryn Fraley, who would come to me every now and then to report something beautiful that had just happened in her involvement with the Southeast Asians. Both agreed to give this visit a try and then almost immediately began wondering why they had said yes. "What can I possibly say to seminary people?" I could only reassure them, "Just hang in there. I believe you're in for a surprise."

And so they made the trip. How well I recall that first evening with Harold in the seminary guest room. That quiet, hopeful conversation and fervent time of prayer, both of us hoping that Kathryn was finding friendly support in the home where she was staying. Both of them came through with flying colors, the "celebrities" of the lecture series, as I had anticipated.

In each session—the chapel services and the informal discussion times—I was the introducer, telling how Harold and Kathryn had gotten into the excitement of an old mainline church opening up to let the Spirit move it from maintenance to mission. Then they would give the specifics, putting "flesh on the bones," "getting the project into work clothes."

Harold was having the last word in this closing chapel service. When he began, "I want to tell you about my journey into compassion," I remember thinking, "Well, that certainly fits." He went on to tell how he had been raised in a Christian home in Western Kansas—born in a sod hut and well acquainted with primitive living conditions. He spoke with deep feeling and some humor about his accepting Christ as a lad of fifteen followed by his baptism in a horse tank brought into the church in Weskan, Kansas. This marked the beginning of a lifelong commitment. Over the years Harold had gone the second mile in doing all the expected in-house church tasks—teaching Sunday School classes, serving as Sunday School superintendent for over twenty-five years, chairing a church building committee, and heading up several stewardship programs, plus serving as a deacon and trustee in a number of churches. He had done it all, even singing in a quartet with three of his brothers.

Now at the end of a long career as a public school teacher and principal, and most recently the manager of an audiovisual store, he and Vivian, his bride of fifty-one years, had come to Wichita to retire from everything, including church work! Of course, they would join some church and participate in worship and give their tithe, but that would be it! Or so they thought!

When they showed up at First Baptist, not only were Harold and Vivian greeted warmly, but they were immediately encouraged to join us in Christ's mission to the city. Every able-bodied, obedient believer was needed, an invitation they couldn't turn down. After a few visits they cast their lot with us, even though they had to drive halfway across the city for anything going on in the church building.

When Harold was asked to serve on the committee responsible for the Deacons' Fellowship Fund, the "cup of cold water" communion offering with which we helped the poor and needy, he wasn't able to say no. After all, that "wouldn't take much time." And when it was suggested at the first meeting that Harold seemed to be the logical one to chair the committee, he could only say, "Well, I guess I can give it a try." That was only the beginning, for later the subject of the "clothing room" was brought up. "Something ought to be done about that room in the north building." A constant source of embarrassment, for it was in such a state of disarray with cast-off clothes dumped in stacks here and there.

If Harold, who wanted things done decently and in order, planned to stay retired, he never should have entered that room in the fall of 1980. What he saw was enough. Any self-respecting church wouldn't dignify that dingy, ill-kept place by calling it a "clothing room." Lots of people had been saying that for some time. The difference between this man and those well-meaning folks was he did something about it! He recruited Vivian, who didn't need much persuading, and a couple of others, and went to work cleaning up the place, carefully sorting through the clothes, and hanging up all that was usable in neat order. Then he established some regular times when people could come and be clothed, as Harold put it, "in the spirit of Jesus."

Now an excitement began to fill that place. Something new was going on there. Our church folks began rummaging through their closets, bringing in usable, clean clothes. And all kinds of needy people, who have an amazingly reliable grapevine, began showing up. "You can find good clothes at First Baptist." This mission of mercy grew beyond all our expectations.

It was all a bit like that experience recorded in the Acts of the Apostles. When that newborn, growing body of believers heard the complaints of those Greek widows being neglected in the daily distribution, they moved to care for their needs. They chose men of "good repute, full of the Spirit and of wisdom" (Acts 6:3) to minister to the poor. It seemed the Lord had led us to such a man. Now seventy-six years of age, Harold had surely earned his retirement. But he had been drawn into a ministry of mercy from which he could not turn away. As he put it, "I needed no manual of procedure. I used my own experience from other areas of organizing." The Holy Spirit was filling him with love and gifting him for this ministry to which he had been called. This always happens for those who dare to obey.

And he never could have done it without Vivian—that joyful, optimistic teammate the Lord had given him. They were game to take on any challenge, it seemed. And others joined in, rounded up by the Lord—beautiful, loving people with a heart for the poor—George and Evelynn Boal, neighbors and intimate coworkers; Thelma Friesen, Kathryn Fraley, Judy Woods, and Chet Dine in those early days, and later a couple of enthusiastic, vibrant women, Jessie Brooks and Orpha Trugillo. As time went on, others came, too numerous to mention.

This whole fledgling venture, into which Harold and his crew were moving with such zest, made me aware again of a central spiritual axiom. Whenever someone sees a need and says, "That has my name on it, a calling from the Lord which I can't turn down," the Spirit will gift and empower that person for that mission. And others will join in! They become the Lord's taskforce, neither too large nor too small, moving out to tackle a divine opportunity. Gideon and his small army of 300 defeating the Midianites; Jesus and the Twelve going forth to proclaim the Kingdom; Paul with Silas and Timothy and Luke crossing over into Europe; John Perkins and the Voice of Calvary reviving life in Mendenhall, Mississippi; Gordon and Mary Cosby and that pioneering colony of heaven in Washington, D.C. called The Church of the Saviour. But can an "ordinary" church know this joy and excitement, this contagion of renewal? Yes, it can, wherever a few expectant souls dare move out knowing Jesus has invited them to heal the sick and proclaim the kingdom.

But how often it has been otherwise. Yes, the need is there and the invitation has been issued. But we hang back, fearful and disobedient. "Yes, I admit the need is great and we ought to do something about it. But where is the money coming from?" So often the first consideration. "And we don't have anyone who can take it on." "Don't ask me—I simply couldn't do it. That's not my kind of thing. Furthermore, I don't have the time."

All too often I have heard that dismal kind of refrain in some church committee or board meeting. So we miss the opportunity. We would rather organize another committee or vote to discuss it at the next meeting. So church life becomes dull and tasteless, apathetic and unexpectant. We have settled for maintenance rather than mission. No wonder the eager ones, the dreamers, so often leave the established church for the nondenominational or Pentecostal churches, which too often we have wrongly criticized. They leave because they feel a slow death has set in and they would rather be where there is some kind of life.

But at Old First this work of mercy grew. Wichita had more people existing on the edge of poverty, even living on the streets, than any of us had imagined. One of the Sunday School classes, the Amicus-Fidelis, turned over their small food pantry to Harold and his team. By now the room in the north building had become crowded beyond capacity. So, late in 1983 the whole operation was moved to far more spacious quarters on the fourth floor of the south building, easily accessible by the elevator off Second Street. This center of hope became known as The Trading Post. A fitting name, because it was a place of exchange, where gracious giving and receiving could take place. Strangers coming, vulnerable and needy, being received as friends, leaving more with us than they ever realized, reminding us of our own helplessness and dependency.

But our own church people "traded" there too. Some of our younger couples were delighted to often find clothing for their small children. One day when I told our associate pastor's wife how attractive her dress was, she responded, "Oh, yes, it's the best. I got it at The Trading Post."

And the demand kept growing. At times it was almost overwhelming—that sad procession of hungry, ragged people coming our way. Proud, gifted folks, most of them eager to work if given half a chance. Often entire families, some transients, black and white, brown and red, old and young, often carrying a sleeping child, patiently waiting their turn outside The Trading Post. An army of neglected, hurting people, so often overlooked and forgotten when the government boasts optimistically about all those new jobs that have been created. And this in the heart of a breadbasket state which usually reports a wheat harvest of 400 million bushels in a normal year.

More than once I have come on someone nervously scrounging for some scrap of food in the garbage can in the alley alongside the church, particularly the morning after a supper at the church.

This church, which had once been a "chaplain to the power structure" in the community, now found itself becoming a servant to the city, going through a gradual but very real conversion. One could catch intimations of this in the warm, friendly way our receptionist greeted the needy people coming our way. And our folks were not turned off when they came on these friends using our restrooms or drinking fountains or wandering the halls trying to find The Trading Post, or even when some of them gathered for a smoke at the Second Street entrance. Yes, they could be messy and they smelled somewhat different than most middle class people. But more and more of our congregation seemed to understand these folks were being sent by the Lord. And when we dared treat them with dignity and respect, sharing what we could, we were surprised by the presence of the One who promised to meet us in the "least of these."

Of course there was no way we could avoid being "conned" now and then. Once a church begins to open its life, it will be played for a sucker. This should not alarm us. For in a strange and wondrous sense our Lord became the biggest Sucker of all on our behalf. "God shows His love for us in that while we were yet sinners Christ died for us" (Romans 5:8). We discovered, for example, that some who had gotten clothes from The Trading Post banded together in sponsoring a garage sale. The free gifts were being sold for a price. So it became necessary to develop some simple guidelines, keeping a record of the clothes each person received and limiting each one to five garments four times a year.

And word got out among our friends at neighboring St. John's Episcopal Church who called, "Could you use some more clothes?" "Of course!" "Well, we've been giving our clothes to another church which makes a small charge for what is passed on, and we want these clothes to be given away with no strings attached." The next day they almost overwhelmed us by bringing a small truckload of beautiful clothes, much of it fit for a party. And that was only the beginning, for they came again and again.

At the heart of it all was this gentle, caring man and his cheerful companion. His arms so often folded, at times looking like he was about to fall asleep, but always dreaming, pushing out, enlarging the ministry; always becoming more and more an advocate for the poor; quietly asking every now and then, "When can we have another food Sunday? The pantry is almost empty again." So at first it was once a year, then three or four times a year, when he would stand up before the congregation to make an appeal. And the vision spread. The congregation became increasingly involved, praying for the ministry, asking how they could help, and having lots of fun on those "food Sundays." What a sight on those special days to see all kinds of people—young and old, often whole families—coming across the parking lot carrying their sacks, scores of them, filled with the basics of life.

But even that was not enough. So Harold turned to the Kansas Food Bank, a great volunteer effort launched largely by the chief executive officer of Boeing's huge Wichita plant. And one day he announced, as excited as a child with a shining new bicycle, "We're now getting all kinds of canned goods for six cents a pound." Even though later that had to be raised to ten cents, it was still a marvelous bargain.

Excellent records were kept. For example, in 1987, 9,696 individuals came, 3,552 of them in families, asking for clothing, and 16,316 items were given them in the name of Christ, much of it for infants and children. And all who came hungry were given food. That same year 6,740 individuals and 2,392 families left carrying those precious sacks. And there was no end to the financial needs—the gas had been turned off, or the family was about to be evicted, or Dad's job had been terminated, or there was an urgent need to get to Tulsa or Dallas or Kansas City and the gas tank was empty. Our people gave hundreds of dollars every month to the Deacons' Fellowship Fund to meet those kinds of needs, often for our own people.

And at the end what a surprise for Harold, who thought he had come to Wichita to retire. As he said in that chapel service at Northern, "I had done all those necessary church tasks over the years. But now in these last years Christ has come alive for me in a fresh, new way, among the poor. I have met Him among the least of these." Then he concluded his witness, so quietly and tenderly, "I used to be curious about the poor. Now I love them." No wonder the dean was wiping his eyes—so was I.

But was giving out sacks of groceries, even in a personal way, enough? Perhaps there was the possibility of a deeper relationship with these people? So many of them were lonely and discouraged, down on life. Thus we began to wonder out loud if there might not be another open door here, inviting these friends to join us for a hot meal once a week. Then we might get to know them a bit, not as people with problems, but as friends. Harold thought that was something we ought to try. We certainly had the facilities and an enthusiastic, cooperative kitchen crew. But did we have the heart for it, the will to tackle such a venture?

Think of all those fascinating conversations and life-changing encounters Jesus had with friends over food. With His close friends Martha, Mary, and Lazarus in Bethany; with Zaccheus, who crawled down from his perch so hastily, hardly daring to believe Jesus had invited Himself to his house for a meal; with Matthew, so elated about his decision to leave his tax-collecting business that he invited his friends in for a meal to meet his new Master—"bad characters," the religious leaders called these friends. Yes, Jesus was always eating with someone.

And what about the feast of bread and fish Jesus spread for that great throng of 5,000 men with their families? He was not using bread to pick up some new disciples, but fed them because they were hungry and He had compassion on them. Wasn't that our situation? Here were hungry people coming our way day after day like sheep without a shepherd.

The "fellowship of eating" can be a profoundly sacramental event—a time of friendship and bonding, as food and conversation are mingled. We are on common ground, regardless of what may divide us, when our hunger is being satisfied. Here that prayer our Lord taught us, "Give us this day our daily bread" (Matthew 6:11), is being answered.

So we raised the question at our next board meeting. Perhaps we were being called to invite hungry people to join us for a meal once a week, not dealing with them in a handout fashion, but as friends? Our kitchen people had already indicated they were willing to give it a try. The board almost immediately approved this new venture—believed it was right—"if we could finance it." But how? Our church budget was stretched to the breaking point. Of course, we could always take another offering, but not from our "regulars" who were already involved in all the special offerings they could handle.

Well, there was another group that might be interested in helping out—our Tuesday noon Bible study group. At least we could ask them.

That Bible study was another one of those "surprises." Two men, Dick Coe and Tom Ward, had gently encouraged us to launch a downtown Bible study. Central Christian, which had been carrying on such a study, had moved out to the suburbs. This left a "noontime vacuum" for a strong core of men. I put Dick and Tom off as long as I could. First Baptist was not Central Christian, and I had more irons in the fire now than I could handle without taking on anything more. So I thought. But when they came to the office asking me one more time, I agreed to pray about it and talk it over with our church leaders. Their response was, "Sounds like a good idea. If you have the time, maybe you should give it a try."

So we did! Eileen Cowles, our faithful kitchen hostess at the time, agreed to take on another meal, having no idea how many would come. A simple message printed on a plain card was distributed around downtown by Dick and Tom, inviting people to join us for a lunchtime Bible Study on Tuesdays. A light meal would be served from 12:00 to 12:20, followed by a life-centered study from the Gospel of Mark, concluding promptly at 12:50. We hoped whoever came would be strengthened in their life of discipleship.

I remember that first Tuesday—how we all suffered from "pregame jitters" wondering, "Will anyone show?" Eileen could not help asking, "How many shall I prepare for?" All I could say was, "I have no idea. Why don't you get ready for sixty?" Really an inflated number I felt, but better too much than not enough. Roy Lassen and Maurice Porterfield, both retired and sharing willingly of their time wherever needed, agreed to be our "cashiers," followed later by Stuart and Rose Pady, a delightful couple who had retired after a lifetime in the academic community. And a beautiful group, recruited by Vivian Leffingwell, had come to set tables, keep the coffee cups filled, and clean up afterward. Virginia Couchman, an optimistic "veteran," became a fixture in passing out the water glasses as the men came by cafeteria style. She greeted many of them by first names and was sorely missed when she couldn't make it.

Our "first customer" was greeted in royal style. At least one had come. But then there was the sound of others coming down the stairs. To our delight, fifty-three came, and I would have settled for a dozen.

And there was a spirit of anticipation in the air, like, "We can hardly wait to see what is going to happen here today." As I stood to share from the Gospel that day, I could sense this was the Lord's doing. Another door of ministry had been opened here at the center of the city. And that was only a foretaste of what was to come. The word spread. The next week there were seventy-two on hand, and within a few weeks we were averaging between 180 and 200 as our gatherings opened up to include the women who were eager to join us. Many brought their fellow-workers, and in a few cases whole offices of employees showed up. So they came— Roman Catholics, Methodists, Pentecostals, Presbyterians, many seekers, and even a few Baptists. What a procession! The sight of John Eberhardt, a venerable, white-haired attorney reported to be an agnostic in earlier days, coming with three or four of his younger colleagues, like a father with his sons, would always give me a lift. He would stop by as he was leaving to speak a warm word of encouragement, "You really got it said today," or "Man, that was some lesson."

Every Tuesday I would come down from my study like a boy eager to open a great package at Christmas, wondering, "Will they be here again today?" And they were. I never got over that quiet, expectant hush when I stood to teach. It was one of the most refreshing, renewing times of the week.

Now and then a man would ask, as casually as possible, if we could spend a bit of time together, but usually there was a hidden urgency in his request. And often those visits became times of confession and healing. "I've been 'ratting' on my wife, and I can't go on this way any longer." "I'm using entirely too much alcohol." "I literally hate my boss." "I've been in a church for a long time, but how can I get started with Christ?" These became holy, sacred sessions. What a wonder to see a man leave the office rejoicing in Christ — forgiven and set free!

It was to this group I turned for help. Would they be willing to pick up the tab so that we might begin feeding hungry people every Friday in the name of Christ? We hoped to serve a good meal for a dollar a person. At this point we had everything but the money. Anything they shared must be completely voluntary. There was immediate and spontaneous approval, "We're glad we can help." It was almost as if they had been waiting for something like this.

The next week our first offering was received, in as low-key a manner as we could manage. "There's a bread basket at each table. If you feel right about sharing something to feed hungry people, simply put something in, large or small." We were amazed to discover that a little over $1,100 had been left. Later that week a woman whom I hardly knew quietly handed me a piece of paper. "I want to help with your feeding program." I thanked her, slipped it into my coat pocket, and forgot it until I undressed that evening. To my delight I found it was a check for $500. Once again it seemed the Lord was taking our loaves and fish, blessing and multiplying them, that the multitude might be fed.

But with what spirit would we serve the hungry who came our way? Reluctantly and condescendingly, or with tenderness and warmth? Perhaps not only the bread and fish were blessed that day Jesus lifted up those humble gifts, but also the disciples, who were filled with a new spirit of gratitude and expectancy as they carried those overflowing baskets out among the hungry. Was not our situation a bit like theirs? There was One among us not only blessing and multiplying what we hoped to share, but filling us with His spirit of anticipation and hospitality, even before we had gotten underway. Our kitchen was becoming more and more this kind of place.

Eileen Cowles had served unselfishly as the church kitchen hostess for eighteen years, often going beyond the call of duty. All of us had enjoyed her sticky cinnamon rolls and that special fried chicken she served on certain occasions! But a church kitchen can be a demanding place. One day she informed us, "I may have to give the kitchen up, much as I'd hate to." She agreed to let us know when the time came.

About this time Jim Bowlus came along. His friend Marieta had brought him to church. Greeting him at the door that first time, I couldn't help noticing that quizzical, wondering look about him. He was a seeker and he shared his questions in a number of visits we had. A few weeks later he confessed Christ. Then Marieta and he were married in a simple, joyous celebration.

Jim had been the assistant chef at the Farm Credit Services Cafeteria for only a short time. One Sunday over lunch I almost jokingly suggested, "You know Eileen is having some difficulty with her health and may have to give up the kitchen one of these days. I don't suppose you'd be interested in taking it over." Not at all expecting the answer I got, "You know, I might be interested in that." "Well, I'm sure it would mean less pay and longer hours." But Jim was far more interested than I realized in serving the Lord in some new, fresh way. "Oh, I'm certain Marieta and I could work out something on the money. She has a good job." The next week Eileen handed us her letter of resignation, having no knowledge of this conversation. So Jim became our "Jesus'

Party Boy," not because we wanted to be irreverent, but because every meal can be an occasion of "eating and drinking with Jesus." Calling Jim a cook or host just didn't seem to fit.

In time a beautiful crew of helpers joined Jim in making the kitchen a place of hospitality and laughter: Chem, a lovely Laotian woman whose whole countenance glowed whenever she smiled; Denise, a gentle, childlike person who was the daughter of our Christian Education minister; Cheryl, struggling bravely with M.S. and so grateful she had something meaningful to do; and Jay, who had shown up out of the blue wanting to help, subject now and then to seizures.

Two months after Jim joined us we asked if he were willing to take on preparing a Friday meal for the hungry. Without hesitation he answered, "That's why I'm here. When do we start?" A few weeks later we were underway.

So again we waited that first Friday as we had some years earlier before that first Tuesday luncheon. The invitation had gone out by word of mouth through The Trading Post and the nearby Episcopal Venture House. "If you're hungry, join us Friday for a hot meal among friends." We needn't have been concerned, for come they did. It was almost like Jesus welcoming the halt, the maimed, and the blind. At first thirty or forty, then a few weeks later our "family" had grown to around 200. It was another procession coming down those stairs to be welcomed this time by Maurice Porterfield, or "Port" as we called him, our beloved dollar-a-year man. Often whole families came, with youngsters who literally wolfed their food down, sometimes eating with their hands. As we broke bread and visited with these people, we met men on the move looking for work, hungry and discouraged, some smelling of alcohol, bearing the mark of a hangover, and women who had no idea where "their man" was.

How well I recall sitting by a weary, unshaven man who identified himself as Charley. He had come from Tacoma, moving eastward, hoping for some kind of a break. "Maybe I'd have better luck finding something in Dallas." When I asked, "Where'd you sleep last night?" he answered off-handedly, "In a culvert." No big deal. This had become a way of life for him. And Charley was not an isolated case, only typical of others who would often admit they lived either on the street or in a car. What a shame that well over three million of our fellow citizens — one-fourth of them children — have no place to lay their heads, and their number is growing. In this affluent land, the rich are becoming richer while the poor are becoming poorer.

One of our guests, Joe, would usually sit down at the baby grand piano and make his offering. Beating out strange, dissonant sounds to an erratic rhythm, occasionally half-singing, half-speaking words none of us could understand. The ritual was almost the same every time Joe came. We bantered about this among ourselves. "This is a high-class place. What other eating establishment has live entertainment while lunch is being served?"

These friends seemed relieved when we did not "preach at them," but simply welcomed them and offered a prayer of thanks because all these gifts came from our Lord. We let them know we were available if they wanted to visit.

Week after week a cheerful, hope-filled company would show up to keep the ministry going. There was always something special about the way these folks dished up the food while they greeted our guests, as if they had known them all their lives. Max Dobbins and Bob Witherspoon, now retired, had driven over from the west side, excited to be working together. Longtime friends out of touch for years, they had discovered at a high school reunion they lived within a few blocks of each other. Max had invited Bob to "his" church and so he and Dee found a new spiritual home among us. Bob Neff had hurried over from his lumberyard to spend his lunch hour among these hungry people, serving and encouraging them. He claimed this was about the best thing he did all week. And there was Port, filling the water glasses and making sure there was enough coffee for everyone, and, of course, Harold, seeing that things were properly organized.

There were many others, but these were the backbone of our crew.

Every so often one of our guests would give us a boost. "You know I like coming here. You treat us like real people."

Through all this we were being stretched and challenged and taught, learning once again that "the Word became flesh and dwelt among us" (John 1:14). He had lived here knowing the pain and joy, laughter and tears, temptation and rejection—as we do. Born of a woman, struggling in a carpenter shop to put bread on the table; baptized with sinners like us in a dirty river; teaching and healing the lame and the possessed, the blind and the leper; feeding the hungry and even saving a wedding party from embarrassment when the wine ran out; turning sorrow into joy by calling Lazarus forth to life; finally dying, thirsty and bleeding, in shame at a place little better than a garbage pile "outside the city gate."

The evidence of His identity as risen Lord for those fearful disciples was His scars, a riven side, and pierced hands. All so earthy and real. But only thus could our salvation be complete. So we who bear His name must join Him "outside the camp, and bear the abuse He endured" (Hebrews 13:13). At least we could grasp this a little better as we joined hungry men and women and children at those tables.

Dare we settle then for a kind of bloodless verbalizing, getting people to "say it our way," or quibbling over some pet theory of biblical inspiration or the details of the second coming? Acting like scribes and Pharisees avoiding the pain and need all around us? Or withdrawing into a frenzied round of activities and programs which have no healing power for those who are hurting and lonely? Or spending our energy fixing roofs and boilers and painting bathrooms as the most important mission of the church? No, we were called to join Jesus in His fleshly ministry "outside the gate." Perhaps we were beginning to hear His claim in a new way.

We also discovered the poor had much to teach us—far more than we had to give them. How easy for us to congratulate ourselves on what we were doing for them, but end up, strangely, being indebted to these who were at our mercy. They came to us so helpless. Life had been stripped to its bare necessities. Yet we often saw in them a gentleness and a childlikeness, a spirit of generosity and patience with adversity, that caused us to know afresh it is the poor in spirit who will inherit the kingdom of God (Matthew 5:3).

At times we found ourselves embarrassed and troubled, not because these who were naked and hungry, sick and thirsty, had come to judge us, but because we were dealing with Another who had said, "As you did it to one of the least of these My brethren, you did it to Me" (Matthew 25:40).

We really are at His mercy. In these who come knocking at our door, He becomes our judge. Do we really need all these trinkets, this heavy baggage we cling to so compulsively? No. Our only hope is to let go. "Go, sell what you have, and give to the poor ... and come, follow Me" (Mark 10:21). "He has put down the mighty from their thrones, and exalted those of low degree" (Luke 1:52).

Those burning, searching words of Studdert Kennedy come to mind:

All eyes was in 'is eyes, — all eyes,
    My wife's and a million more.
And once I thought as those two eyes
    Were the eyes of the London whore.
And they was sad, — My Gawd 'ow sad,
    With tears that seemed to shine,
And quivering bright wi' the speech o' light,
    They said, " 'er soul was mine."
There ain't no throne, and there ain't no books,
    It's 'im you've got to see,
It's 'im, just 'im, that is the Judge
    of blokes like you and me.
And boys, I'd sooner frizzle up,
    I' the flames of a burning 'ell,
Then stand and look into 'is face,
    And 'ear 'is voice say — "Well?"[1]

I am reminded of this every time I open my *New English Bible*. For here at my place of reading is a bookmark, frayed a bit, with "Expect a Miracle," painted on the one side with a special flourish in watercolor, with a heart and flowers done in green, blue, yellow, and silver. All this brightness is so consistent with the words. On the other side is, "Blessed is the man who trusts in the Lord," with a long-stemmed blue flower. This is a special gift from Edith Mott, and is not for sale under any circumstances.

Edith had come to us some years before, so shy she could hardly lift her eyes to greet us, but surely sent by the Lord. Her clothes revealed her creative flair, always different and colorful.

One day she surprised me by asking softly if she might be baptized. When I suggested I would be delighted to come by her home to visit about this, she immediately insisted she would rather meet at the church. I was a bit mystified the day she came in, when she brought out a sheet of blue paper and began writing on it as soon as she was seated. All during our visit—and I discovered Edith did know Christ as her Saviour and understood baptism as a confession of our dying and rising to new life in Him—she kept writing. There was no way I could deny her eagerness to be baptized on Easter Sunday. As she left Edith gave me that blue piece of paper. I was somewhat taken aback at the portrait of me that Edith had sketched.

Easter Sunday came. When I asked those being baptized if any of them had a fear of the water, they all assured me there was no problem. But when Edith entered the water I could see a look of anxiety in her eyes. As I began to lower her under the water as gently as possible, after hearing her witness to her faith in Jesus Christ, she began to resist. It would have been utterly wrong to have forced her immersion, but as I released her, she did the unexpected—stepped to the other end of the unusually large baptistry, bent forward, and lowered her head under the water, literally baptizing herself! I could only utter the words of the baptismal confession in amazed wonder, "I baptize you, Edith, in the name of the Father, the Son, and the Holy Spirit." There was a holy hush as she left the water. Then I heard myself saying, "How wondrously Edith has blessed us by insisting that she obey our Lord's command, in spite of her fear of the water." Joyous, reverent "Amens" echoed through the sanctuary. That may well have been the central affirmation of that Resurrection service.

After the service, Edith's mother, whom I had never met, gratefully sought us out. "This is the first church that has 'made anything' over Edith. She feels at home here."

And Edith blessed us in all kinds of surprising ways — helping with children's crafts in our Vacation Bible School, or leaving her colorful markers with a word of Scripture at each woman's place for one of their luncheons, much to their delight. "Look what Edith has done again!" And often I have gotten a special lift receiving one of her unusual birthday greetings — four or six pages of flowers, birds, angels, and butterflies done in striking colors.

How much poorer we would have been if this dear woman had not shown up and then overcome her hesitation by joining God's people. "The parts of the body which seem to be weaker are indispensable" (1 Corinthians 12:22).

Little by little our family at Second and Broadway began to understand the rich meaning of the "word becoming flesh." The spirit of hospitality and caring began to seep into our congregational life. Those hardy, faithful, generous souls who welcomed all who came to The Trading Post and served the lunches on Tuesdays and Fridays had a quiet, leavening effect on the rest of the body. There was a contagion about what they were experiencing and learning that touched all of us. Somehow those apostolic phrases — "Do not neglect to show hospitality to strangers, for thereby some have entertained angels unawares" (Hebrews 13:2); "If one member suffers, all suffer together; if one member is honored, all rejoice together" (1 Corinthians 12:26); "forbearing one another and, if one has a complaint against another, forgiving each other"

(Colossians 3:13)—began to describe our life together. We were joining Harold on that journey into compassion, some cautiously, some fearfully, others eagerly. But there was no turning back.

Will You Join Jesus?

Are there any cries for help where you are?—some hidden and silent, but others that almost shout at you? Do you hear them? An alcoholic, desperate and sick of life, hiding behind drawn blinds down the street? That faithful woman you see in church week after week barely making it on a limited fixed income, too embarrassed to let anyone know her roof is leaking and the furnace needs repair? That hungry man who showed up at the church needing food and some gas for his aging car—he was the fourth one this week—how easy to treat him as an interruption? The Smiths, trying so hard to keep a stiff upper lip, going off to visit their son in the penitentiary, picked up for armed burglary and high on drugs? That tired young mother you see coming and going, struggling to hold down a job and somehow care for three growing children? Fleshly, basic needs right under our noses. And yet we can pass by, even on the other side of the road.

Is it really enough just to have another discussion about these kinds of needs? To carefully analyze what the Bible has to say about our responsibility for the poor and dispossessed, the hungry and the ill? To again pass a resolution which proposes that somebody—government agency or whoever—should come up with a solution? Name yet another committee to deal with it? Or pray about it and assume that's taken care of the need? Is this the best we can do? If that is all, then we cannot expect any kind of renewal to come our way.

Or dare we listen to these cries for help, believing the Word can become flesh through us? What does that mean? Well, it at least means watching Jesus and learning from Him, moving as He did among the lepers, the hungry, the naked, the crippled, and the possessed—the ones who knew they needed a physician! He did not minister at a distance, but intimately and personally. He gave Himself, taking the leper by the hand, touching the eyes of the blind with His own spit, lifting up the crippled, confronting the evil spirits in the possessed, and feeding the hungry. That's all you can do—give yourself!

But we say we do not have the resources. He says, "I will take whatever you offer Me, bless it, and minister to those in need." When He confronted that great hungry crowd of 5,000 after teaching them for a day, some of His disciples said, like we do, "Send them away; we can't handle this." Another one counted up the money and said they couldn't even get started with this pittance. And Andrew brought a lad who had only some dark, coarse bread and some minnows. That's all, but for Jesus it was more than enough!

This is the miracle of Mother Teresa helping the wretchedly ill die with dignity in the love of Jesus; of Keith Phillips being drawn into the ghetto in Watts and launching a movement known as World Impact that is now helping to heal the physical and spiritual and emotional hurts of some of the major cities in America; of Chuck Colson bringing life and hope to a multitude of hardened criminals in prisons all over the world through Prison Fellowship. You may say, "These are all well-known names." But they are ordinary people who obeyed. Then started small and promptly. So can you!

Sit down with a group of fellow pilgrims and simply ask, "Where are the needs and when will we start?" Not a "do good" project to soothe your conscience, but a move to join Jesus in His ministry to the world. Yes, there will be strain and tension in the church fellowship—"We've never done anything like that before. Why get involved now?" But new life never comes without birth pangs.

Chapter Seven

No Longer Strangers

*"For He is our peace, who has
made us both one." Ephesians 2:14*

It was a phone call that brought our people into the painful
world of the refugee. Matt Giuffrida, our denominational director of refugee settlement, a quietly compassionate, but
tenacious man with an unsurpassed record for finding homes
for displaced people, was calling from New York City. A Cambodian family, the Chin Saloeuns—father, mother, two daughters aged seven and one, and Chin's father—desperately
needed someone to sponsor them. Matt had checked all his
available leads with no success and the family had to be
moved by morning. Would we be willing to take them?

How providential that Dick Worley, our associate pastor,
should take that call. He and Charlotte had joined our staff
after seventeen years in Thailand as evangelistic and educational missionaries. Enthusiastic and fun-loving, they brought
a spirit of excitement and adventure to our congregation. And
they had the world on their hearts, particularly the people of
Southeast Asia.

So when Dick came charging into my office that Wednesday evening just before our fellowship supper and prayer
service, there was no way of holding him back. He was utterly convinced that phone call was the Lord's doing. We would
regret it forever if we turned aside from this opportunity

being given us. Since we had to give Matt some kind of answer by morning, there wasn't much chance to call the board together for official approval.

All we could do was share this call for help with our prayer meeting crowd and see how they responded. So after our Bible study, just before our time of prayer, Dick very simply laid the issue before the people. A Cambodian family of five was waiting in New York City for some word of hope. Could there be a new beginning for them somewhere after those long, wearying months in the refugee camp? Would we be willing to risk sponsoring them? This meant far more than signing some papers and then letting the family fend for themselves. If we took this step, the family would be "ours" — like adopted children. We would be finding a place for them to live and furnishing it with dishes, bedding, and all the rest; then helping them find work, getting the children to school, and introducing them to our "strange" American ways. But most important, we would be loving these people as friends.

Our people heard all this and understood. Their answer was a strong "Yes." They would welcome and make a home for this family. Our prayers following that decision were quite fervent and specific.

A couple of days later we gathered at the airport to wait for the arrival of "our family" — a nervous, excited welcoming committee wondering how it would all work out. Then the plane arrived and they were coming up the walkway, five small, gentle people whose weariness from the long journey could not hide the bright hope shining in their eyes. And how polite they were. We bowed, shook hands, and smiled trying to bridge the culture and language gaps that divided us, hoping they felt welcome. Dick and Charlotte Worley, who spoke Thai fluently, assured us they did. The adventure had begun. That day those stirring words on the base of the Statue of Liberty — "Give me your tired, your poor, your huddled masses yearning to breathe free" — took on fresh meaning.

The spontaneous decision made to sponsor that first family

opened the door to a world of alienation and homelessness from which we could not turn aside. It almost seemed as if the spiritual wounds our people had suffered in earlier years made them particularly sensitive to these strangers who came knocking at our door. Before it was all over, this church in Wichita, Kansas, half a world away from wartorn Southeast Asia, sponsored twenty-four other families, altogether 131 people—Vietnamese, Laotians and Cambodians. Everyone who came to us seemed to have a mother, a grandfather, a husband, or a family member waiting month after month for someone to sponsor them so that they too could have a new beginning. We did not have to go to them. They were coming to us. And our people were being given the grace to keep saying, "Welcome."

We were to hear all kinds of heartwrenching stories from these new friends, like when Nguyen Dinh Chien, a trained civil engineer, let us in on a bit of his costly flight to freedom. We listened almost breathlessly, not wanting to miss a word, as he spoke in his soft, broken English. Fifty-three of them had escaped from Vietnam by night, setting out in their homemade boat, which they had secretly nailed together over months with bits and scraps scrounged in camp. A few miles out, to their horror, one of the two engines failed—the big one. Now they had to hastily change plans and head straight west for Malaysia, almost certain the small engine could not carry them that distance. This meant moving into waters constantly patrolled by the Communists who would surely kill them, as they had so many others. To their amazement they encountered no patrol boats and the little engine held out. Chien concluded with tears, "That's why I say God saved us."

Somehow we had to get organized. We couldn't handle this influx of families in a hit-or-miss fashion. There was too much at stake. So a few eager, courageous souls responded to the invitation to help out. Among these were Jeanne Cleaver, a nurse who had earlier been involved with international students; her husband, Ed, director of the Sedgwick

County Public Health office; Vic and Elaine Evans, whose home was always open to all kinds of people; Ruth Covington, constantly reaching out to people on the fringes of society; Sharon Moody, a compassionate, tender seeker finding fulfillment in giving herself to others; and Kathryn Fraley, able to quietly handle all kinds of details with patience.

These turned out to be a special breed, combining an amazing blend of toughness and tenderness, of patience and ingenuity. They had to "wheel and deal" in the spirit of Christ—trusting they were being "wise as serpents and harmless as doves," taking on situations that were utterly new to them, constantly asking for special help from all kinds of public officials. Time and again they had to go to the congregation asking if there were people who still had beds and linens, dishes and used furniture they were willing to share, or if there were those willing to serve as host families or teachers of English, or did anyone know of another job opening someplace.

Dick Worley was a model and encourager in all this. He, along with Charlotte, brought a world of experience and an exhilarating spirit of optimism to this fledgling venture. They seemed to have an ingenious, God-given capacity for pulling the right string at the right time or seeing just the right person when it counted the most.

Like arranging for Prawit Chen, whom we called Peter, to have a kidney transplant which most people said was out of the question. Peter and his wife, Chemtana or Jeannie to us, were a younger, prominent couple doing well in business in Thailand. But he was dying by inches with a major kidney disorder and no adequate medical help available. To Dick that meant only one thing—get Peter to Wichita for a transplant. But there was no way that could be done without $50,000 in hand, so the hospital administrator at St. Francis bluntly turned down the request. All the Chens could do was go home and wait for the end.

But Dick refused to take that as the last word. Surely God would provide a way. He had not allowed Peter and Jeannie to come this far only to be turned down. All this was poured out in prayer in Dick's office. And as he persisted he found the Lord's angel right in the middle of things. A hospital counselor was moved to contact a concerned, determined Social Security worker who literally spent hours sifting through a maze of regulations and finally came on one that opened the door. Peter had been employed briefly in Chanute and Emporia some years earlier while attending school and had paid a small amount into Social Security. That was enough!

Some days later Dick received an urgent call shortly after midnight. A kidney was available. So in the wee hours he drove this excited, hopeful couple to St. Francis and waited with Jeannie during the suspenseful hours of surgery. Which was successful! Peter had been given new life.

But a deeper life came to these two when they confessed Christ. This was not a "payoff" for kindness, but a thoughtful, wholehearted surrender to Jesus as Lord. Jeannie had been strongly anti-Christian in Thailand, but the love poured out on them by the people at First Baptist penetrated her defenses so she could no longer resist the claim of the Great Lover. They are now active members of the Hope Baptist Church in Los Angeles, rejoicing in a flourishing silk flower business, thankful they have been able to share a sizeable gift for a new Christian witness in Thailand.

No wonder Dick was able to write, "That's another story of God's amazing ways." He always expected miracles to take place.

When this group dealing with internationals first met, they could not help being contagiously affected by Dick's kind of working faith. They decided to call themselves the "No Longer Strangers Taskforce," inspired by Paul's beautiful description of the Ephesian Christians. "Now you are no longer strangers to God and foreigners to heaven, but you are members of God's very own family, citizens of God's country, and you belong in God's household with every other Christian" (Ephesians 2:19, TLB). It was the loving hospitality these "strangers" discovered among the people of First Baptist that led many of them to enter into the reality of becoming "members of God's very own family."

That group was delighted whenever public officials greeted them in a friendly, helpful way. For they can become coldly professional, even hardened, dealing with one difficult case after another. Kathryn Fraley, who found herself running a kind of international taxi service getting people to school and to the health and immigration authorities, spoke of this: "I had never really appreciated how much difference a smile can make until I began taking large groups to the Health Department. A nurse who didn't resent refugees and was gentle with the mother and frightened children was a real gift to us all.

"I shall never forget taking one large family with six school-aged children to the Health Department for school physicals. Their blood tests showed they were so anemic that the doctor wondered that one of the little girls was able to stand. He was so kind to us even though we were still there at 5:45. He was so concerned that he made appointments at his office for the next morning for the entire family even though it was his day off. The next day he arranged for an immediate transfusion for Pheung, the little girl with the paper-white skin."

But there was also another kind of response. There was more angry prejudice around than we had imagined, a kind of irrational fear and defensiveness that could erupt in ugly ways. We were embarrassed and shamed when one of our new friends reported, with some hesitation and pain, that neighbors had rubbed dirty diapers on her apartment doorknobs and that later a youngster had come up to her in a laundromat and spit in her face. But there was no bitterness in her voice as she spoke of this, only gratitude for the opportunity being given her. Another family, so eager to show off their newly purchased car—their first one—had come out the next morning to find all the windows broken. But they quietly paid their high-risk insurance, repaired the windows, moved elsewhere, and kept going.

We had much to learn from these tender, forgiving people

who had already suffered so much. How ironic that some Americans would treat them with contempt and fear when we had fought a bloody, tragic war presumably to help them stay free. And how desperately urgent it is that the church recover its mission of reconciliation and healing that it might be Christ's sign to the world of God's intention for the whole human family.

Often we came to know very intimately the pain of a particular family torn asunder by the upheaval in Vietnam. Mrs. Hai Thi Tran came to us with her five children, ages sixteen to twenty-three, almost certain she would never see her husband and daughter alive again. Then word came by way of relatives that they had somehow managed to escape Vietnam by boat. But weeks of anxious waiting followed with no news. During that time Hai would often come to the church asking us to join her in prayer, desperately afraid her husband and daughter had been eaten by a big fish.

Then a telegram came with news almost too good to be true! Her prayers had been answered. The two had landed safely in southern Thailand. They had managed to survive the ordeal of being at sea twenty days, the last six without food and water. Most of those in the boat were unconscious, near death, when they were discovered. But they were alive.

However, the waiting continued to drag on over the next five months while her husband and daughter were transferred from the police station to the refugee camp, and finally to Bangkok. Again a time of anxiety and hope. But along the way there were unexpected "angels," Christian friends who offered encouragement helping them with the endless details of immigration. Finally the last hurdle was cleared and they were on their way.

On April 6, 1979, the plane carrying these two very special people touched down at Midcontinent Airport. There were misty, shining eyes and feelings too deep for words all around the welcoming circle as we watched this dear family greet one another with shouts of joy. All inhibitions were swept aside as the pent-up emotions of the years erupted—the daughter falling into the arms of her mother and the husband and wife clinging to each other—now together after four long, uncertain years of separation.

Even though most of these newcomers were Buddhists or ancestor worshipers, at least in name, they wanted to know about our faith. The songs we sang, the book called the Bible we referred to all the time, and this Jesus we talked about— what did it all mean? So the Taskforce launched a simple Sunday School. A short time was spent each Sunday introducing them to some peculiar American expressions. The way we greet each other, for example. "How are you doing?" "Nice day, isn't it?" "Glad to see you." Or simply, "Hi." And they were wide open to the deeper meanings of the Bible story which was taught each week. But they got the greatest lift joining in on the hymns and praise choruses which they picked up very quickly and sang with such uninhibited enthusiasm they put us old Christians to shame.

The thirty who first came spread the word and the Sunday School grew. The assembly room was soon bursting at the seams, particularly with children. So when San Jittawait, who was in charge of the school, went to the Christian Education division to present this happy situation, Ed Friesen, the chair, asked, "How can we help?" Without hesitation San answered, "We need Bibles and more space." Ed responded immediately, "I'll buy the Bibles, and have you ever thought about moving the Sunday School to the North Building?" That suggestion caught on and the group agreed to check it out.

It was almost as if that old building had been standing there for years, with only the first floor and gym being used, waiting for someone to come and fill it with song and prayer and talk of the Lord.

So the move was made, but not without some hard work and buckets of hot, soapy water. The place was dirty, the heating and air conditioning were questionable, and the water pressure for the restrooms and fountains was low. But as one person put it, "We felt we could overcome all the difficulties for the sake of more space." And they did! It was a happy day when that building, like a gracious, older lady, found her youth again. For Sunday after Sunday 100 or more eager, vibrant Southeast Asians would climb the stairs to take over the second floor with joyous sounds of praise and prayer and study. Now they had a great assembly room with classrooms to spare.

Again the Lord called forth workers—gifted, caring people willing to teach. Mary Porterfield, who had worked with Girl Scouts for more than twenty years, visited the International Sunday School just as it was getting underway. She was intrigued by what she found and continued to attend. She said, "I felt a real sense of warmth, and the desire of the refugees to learn about Christianity was apparent."

Mary ended up joining the others as a teacher; San and Sineerat led the singing; Gayle Holt, our associate pastor's wife, played the piano; Kathryn Fraley and Claudia Sandford taught. Then others came on board! Janice Bear Lawrence, an artist, assisted by Ruby Lawrence—related in Christ, but not by blood—who had given most of her life serving in a seminary; Joy Wilson, a radiant homemaker, assisted by Terry and Diane Lincoln, who were there whenever they were not working at the county zoo. All these were "given to the task of teaching." And there was Rose Pady, who could have easily begged off because of her age, but came eagerly every Sunday to play the piano and teach after Gayle Holt left.

When the Lord pours out His Spirit on a people, they are given "dreams and visions." So declares the Prophet Joel. Surely that was true the night San Jittawait shared his hopes with our church leaders one Monday in the late summer of 1981. He wondered if the time had not come for the Internationals to worship together occasionally in the chapel. There would be far more freedom and participation if they were using a familiar language, probably Thai. The few who had been attending our "regular services" were struggling to understand what was taking place. If the Internationals were to have "their own" Sunday worship they could join us in the sanctuary once a month to celebrate the Lord's Supper. They would not be a separate congregation, but a worshiping "unit" of the whole body meeting at Second and Broadway.

There was immediate response, positive and unanimous. With one mind and heart we then moved to the chapel to join in prayer that the Lord would pour out His Spirit on these people as they began gathering there each Sunday to worship. We felt the Lord was about to do a new thing.

Which He did! Beyond our expectations! Our church paper called that first Sunday, September 27, "A Miracle among the Internationals." One sentence summed it up: "In a wonderful way God honored the faithfulness of all those who had labored with these dear people over the last years." After songs of praise, Scripture, and prayer, James Holt shared the message. James and Gayle Holt had joined our staff succeeding the Worleys, who had gone back to Thailand after three years with us. The Holts, who had served a term as missionaries in the Philippines, were gifted teachers and encouragers. Here was another one of our Lord's gracious serendipities, having two missionary families, who had both served in Southeast Asia, minister among us for a total of seven years at the very time hundreds of people from that part of the world were streaming into Wichita.

In that first service James very carefully explained what it means to be a Christian in one, two, three fashion using a blackboard with San interpreting. Then he extended an intentionally simple, low-key invitation. If the Spirit was calling anyone to confess Jesus Christ as Lord and Saviour, they could step forward. They could not help wondering if anyone would come. After all, this was their first service and Asians by nature are shy people.

But in spite of these misgivings, the invitation had hardly been spoken before people began to move forward as if they had been waiting for such an opportunity. When it was all over, sixty-two people were standing quietly at the front. And there were ninety in attendance. James and San were utterly amazed. Perhaps these people did not understand what they were doing. So James spelled out the invitation once again. "Are you sure you know what you're doing? Do you realize that by confessing Jesus as Lord, you are giving up your old loyalties to Buddha and renouncing ancestor worship, which is so much a part of your culture? You are now beginning a life of obedient discipleship under a new Master. This means a new way of forgiveness and love. Now you can go back and be seated if you do not understand this. We will still love you." But no one moved! They all stood there—committed and determined, eager to be Christ's disciples.

So San began instructing them in the Christian way! And we praised God, Sunday after Sunday, as most of these new believers made their confession in baptism. Many longtime Christians, who had lost that early glow, were shaken and renewed by their unashamed affirmation of Jesus.

So here was a growing family within our congregation needing shepherding and encouragement. But was there anyone who could be their pastor? Little did we realize that the Lord had been preparing that person right in our midst. For here was San Jittawait with his gifted wife, Sineerat, so enthusiastic about all that was happening among the internationals, freely giving every bit of time to them they could possibly squeeze in. No one else understood the language and culture of these people like they did. And their joyous commitment to the Lord often caused the rest of us to ask about our own faithfulness. The Lord had chosen them for a special work only they could do. All this began to dawn on me when San joined me in calling on a Laotian family. Even asking him to join me in this call was an afterthought.

Bounchop and Doungmala Vilaythong had surprised us by stepping forward at the close of a service in the "big church," as they called it. They were so new and seemed so reticent, but came with such determination, immediately asking if they could be baptized. I could not help wondering if they understood what they had done, so arrangements were made for a visit in their home that week. It was then I thought of San, whom I then knew only casually. Would he come along to make certain we all understood one another? Yes, he would be happy to do this.

San had come to Wichita State University to get a master's degree in Educational Administration, through the help of friends, assuming he would be returning to Thailand to become the director of the Sammuk Christian Academy, where he had taught for a short time. But that hope had been thwarted by those in authority back home. So here he was, gifted and well-trained, hiding his disappointment, while he worked on the cutting floor of a large meat-packing plant, wondering what the Lord really had in store for him. There were probably not too many people with a master's degree on that cutting floor. And Sineerat, his lovely wife, was a critical care nurse at St. Francis Hospital.

It was a memorable call the two of us made. Bounchop and Doungmala and their three children greeted us politely, bowing slightly in typical Asian fashion. They were justifiably proud of their little home and the large TV set which almost dominated the living room. After all, it was theirs!

Over tea and small cakes, the Vilaythongs spoke of their new life in America. They were ambitious and had good jobs. Their children were doing well in school and they were all particularly enthusiastic about the soccer team Bounchop was coaching. They also expressed the hope that other members of their family would be able to join them someday.

Then we got down to the main purpose of our call. Did they understand what this coming forward meant? That salvation is God's gift of grace freely offered which can only be received by faith? Was that their experience? And did they know that baptism bore witness to that experience with Christ? Yes, they understood and they did believe! During this conversation, I became aware that San had the heart of a pastoral evangelist. He was filled with holy enthusiasm as he talked about Jesus and answered their questions in a language I did not understand, but knew in my heart to be the speech of heaven. We concluded with prayer and left rejoicing.

Obviously San loved doing this kind of thing. We started for home in silence. Then San spoke quietly, almost wistfully, "Maybe my mission field is right here. Why should I go back to Thailand when so many people are coming here from the refugee camps? And like the Vilaythongs they are eager to hear about Jesus."

It was as if a vision had been kindled. We found ourselves excitedly discussing what could happen if San were able to spend more time among these people—calling, teaching, and leading worship, even if it were only weekends at the start. Perhaps the church would call him to become Pastor of the Internationals. Surely we could dig up some funds to help with his support. Maybe he should consider enrolling at Central Seminary in Kansas City.

And that is exactly what happened! The congregation had become aware the Lord was doing a new thing among these exiles and pilgrims. These people needed consistent, tender shepherding, and the Lord had been preparing San Jittawait for that work. We could only affirm that by calling him to be Minister to the Internationals. The congregation did come up with a modest amount to support their work. And San did enroll in the seminary.

The next two years became a heavy time for the Jittawait family with San taking off every Monday afternoon immediately following our staff meeting, then returning Friday afternoon to jump into all the demands of the growing international congregation. And Sineerat was putting in a full shift at the hospital every weekend as well as mothering their three gifted, growing children, Jip, Joe, and Jane. She also kept in touch with many of the international folks while San was gone. Their home was a place of warm hospitality with people coming and going all hours of the day and night. Somehow the Jittawaits carried it all with grace and patience. But we breathed a sigh of relief and rejoiced when San was granted his M.Div. and came home for keeps.

Through this time we watched the Lord do wondrous things. We had made a rather cautious investment in the ministry of the Jittawaits. But they were casting out the seed with love and abandon on soil that was amazingly fertile. And the Lord gave the increase. The rest of us talked about witnessing to friends and family and fellow workers. They simply did it, inviting uncles and cousins and neighbors to join in their meetings of worship and fellowship.

We discovered our people had really gotten serious about this ministry the day of San's ordination. His carefully prepared ordination paper had been enthusiastically received by the council, and he had answered their questions with disarming wisdom. The council unanimously recommended that our church proceed with San's ordination, which we did with great anticipation. That service was a joyous celebration—the music, the prayers, the preaching—all of it! Far more than being simply another ordination service, it was really an affirmation of that "new thing" God was doing and the man whom He had called to lead this special work.

And we received an offering, almost a last-minute decision. A Baptist service would hardly be orthodox without receiving some kind of offering. It had dawned on us a few days before the service there would be no better time to undergird this growing work than at San's ordination. But with only a week's notice we wondered if our people would come prepared. The chairman of our diaconate, Roger Fraley, voiced our fondest hopes, "Wouldn't it be wonderful if the people gave $6,000?" Again we were surprised. When we counted what had been received it totaled $9,200. So San came on board full time—a wonderful staff teammate—enthusiastically called "Minister with Internationals" by our congregation. We discovered increasingly how gifted San was, both as pastor and evangelist. He eventually became the associate pastor ministering to all our people.

The response of these people to the claims of Christ was not without a cost which most of us have never had to pay. For many of them were accused by their countrymen of being traitors to their ancestors, turning their backs on their native culture. But they gladly accepted this reproach and alienation for they were now members of a new family, where Jews and Gentiles, slaves and free, Asian and American, have become one in Christ.

This was particularly evident at each Communion service when these who were "no longer strangers" would enter the "big church" to join us at the Lord's table. In the act of eating and drinking when San would speak those holy eucharistic words in Thai, I could not help praising God, for now the whole family was together, not only spiritually but physically.

There came a day when "Mr. Nu," as we called him, joined us at that table to serve the bread and the cup, as a deacon. The congregation had discerned those Christlike qualities of faithfulness and service in Mr. Sath Ngam which marked him for leadership in the church. No one's surrender to Christ spoke more eloquently of "amazing grace" than his. Like John Newton, who gave us that treasured hymn, Mr. Nu had lived a life of licentious rebellion, womanizing and boozing, frequently coming home after one of his drinking bouts to beat his faithful wife, Boualong. She could only hope and pray.

Then one Sunday he was cajoled, almost dragged, to an international worship service. As he later said, "I came with a hangover, full of anger, wondering why I had let people talk me into coming." But our God is full of surprises, for on that day a very special guest had been asked to share his testimony. San had invited one of his seminary classmates to join him for the weekend. Deo Vihieno, coming from one of the Naga tribes in Northeast India, from a people who had turned from their animistic, headhunting ways to a new life of peace and joy in Christ, welcomed this opportunity.

Nu was amazed as he listened. Deo's story was his story! He too had wasted his substance in riotous living and had ended up in a pigpen full of self-pity and despair. Then Deo had heard the glorious Gospel story—almost too good to be true—and had repented and turned toward home to discover the Heavenly Father's gracious welcome. Here he experienced forgiveness and peace and the acceptance of God's family. Now Deo was at the seminary preparing to serve his people back in India.

That word and the life from which it flowed touched Nu in his depths and awakened a spiritual hunger deep within. A week or two later he was back at the service. There followed probing conversations with San. And finally his thoughtful, glad surrender to Christ, a glorious day for all of us. Even his countenance revealed the transformation. The troubled frown gave way to a warm, loving glow. And Boualong, his patient wife, reported with a smile, "Everything's changed now at home. Nu has become so kind! I don't have a different husband, but I have a new one."

Nu's love for the Scriptures became obvious. He was never without his Bible and often would say, "I get up early in the morning to read this book. I just can't seem to find enough time to study it." The baptism of Nu and Boualong was a "hallelujah affair," and one by one the children followed. What a delight to join with him as he prayed in his gentle, melodic language or to hear him make music on his khan, a long-stemmed, hollow, fluted Laotian instrument. He became a bold witness among his own countrymen. When he was sworn in as an American citizen, he asked that his name be changed to James.

When Billy Graham came to Oklahoma City for a crusade, Mr. Nu, San, Jittawait, Ron Rogg, our mayor Bob Knight, and I journeyed down to meet briefly with him to discuss the possibility of a crusade in Wichita. We were warmly received, presented our request, and joined together in prayer, and were even invited to be platform guests for the service that evening. Driving home later that night, Mr. Nu spoke repeatedly of what a wonderful experience it had been. "I never dreamed I would ever meet that great man, Billy Graham. And to think I shook his hand. I don't think I'll ever wash that hand again."

Every now and then this wonderful band of shining believers, "No Longer Strangers," would invite all of us to join them for a meal in our fellowship hall. There was always a delicious feast—egg rolls, fried and sticky rice, special chicken, and all the rest—served with such joy. Then they would present one of their programs for us—singing the new songs of redemption with graceful native dancing presented by some of the beautiful children and young women. With a heartwarming testimony interspersed now and then. Christ made the difference! They thanked the congregation over and over again that we had welcomed them. At some point they would sing one of their favorite contemporary choruses, "In His time . . . He makes all things beautiful in His time. Lord, please show me every day, as you're teaching me Your way, that You do just what You say in Your time."

And this is exactly what God was doing—making all things beautiful in His time.

Whom Do I Need To Include?

"But now in Christ Jesus you who once were far off have been brought near in the blood of Christ" (Ephesians 2:13).

What do these words say to you? What implications are in them for church life? Jesus Christ has opened the way, not only in word and life, but through His incredible self-giving death. In this mighty act of grace He extends the great invitation, not only to the rich and powerful, the religious and sophisticated, but to the maimed and poor, the weak and foolish. The Gentile, unwashed and uncircumcised, is now included as well as the Jew. There are no qualifications, no fine print in the contract, no last-minute disappointments— "After all, this really wasn't for you."

So I am included. I came broken and needy, accepted by faith into the family.

What does all this say about my attitude toward others? About church strategy? Dare the church continue being an introverted, cozy club? No, I can no longer impose restrictions on Christ's gracious invitation, draw lines and exclude people. The doors must be opened, the hidden barriers destroyed, if we are to be faithful to the One who is creating a new humanity. In every living church Peter and Cornelius become brothers in Christ.

Let me be quite specific. I once had terrible hang-ups and reservations, even fears, about Roman Catholics and Pentecostals. Then I met Christ among some of these people and discovered to my amazement the wall was really down. We were in the same family at the foot of the cross. And the same was true at one time about alcoholics as well as the people who were handicapped—as I understood them. Then I discovered how radiant and powerful the witness of a recovering alcoholic who knew Christ could be and the depth and power of the faith among the blind and crippled.

It was really another conversion that is still going on. Little by little Christ has smashed my false pretentions and humbled me as I have learned again how great is His work on Calvary. How utterly unconditional is His invitation and wonderfully diverse is the family He is bringing into His household!

Every church is called to be cleansed of its prejudices, to rearrange its priorities and its agenda. Whom should we include that we are now excluding? How can we reach out—authentically, tenderly, and personally—and welcome these in the name of Christ? The black and the white, the Hispanic and the Asian, the old and the young, the poor and the rich, the troubled and the self-righteous, the stranger and the old-timer—all of them!

"For He is our peace" . . . and we are "no longer strangers" (Ephesians 2:14, 19). Will you be one of those on the "inviting edge" of such a renewal?

Chapter Eight

Capitulation Is the Beginning

*"Force me to render up my sword, and
I shall conqueror be. . . . "* George Matheson

The church lives only when there is a death at its center. Not only our Lord's, who has bought us with His own "precious blood," but our own death. A joyful, bold act of surrender. Capitulation is what our oldest son, Randy, called it. And that over the telephone. When, after the usual pleasantries, he blurted out those familiar words, "Blessed are the meek, for they shall inherit the earth," I could only wonder out loud, "Randy, what in the world has happened to you?" His answer was simple and direct. "I have capitulated to the Lord." I could only breathe a prayer of thanks. Then the rest poured out. "Driving back to Rapid City I picked up a couple of hitchhikers. Interesting fellows, who turned out to be sharp, committed Christians, really 'Jesus people,' hitching back and forth across the country, witnessing to whoever picked them up.

"We really went to the mat. Can you really change the world unless people are changed? And that means coming clean with Jesus, going all the way, seeking first His kingdom. I guess I had been wrestling with that far longer than I realized. We ended up camping out over the weekend. I realized during those hours I couldn't run anymore. My life is really not my own. Even though I don't know where it's going to take me, I turned it all over to the Lord. Then these fellows baptized me in the Grand River. Something deep has happened to me. I know things are going to be different, and I wanted you and Mom to know."

I was utterly silent for a moment, amazed once again at the wondrous ways of our Lord. But a song welled up in my heart. Then I tried as best I could to utter a word of prayerful affirmation and joined Ruth with tears of thanksgiving and praise.

Yes, Randy had been baptized as a boy, perhaps feeling more subtle parental pressure than I realized. But in the years that followed at Washington High School and Yale University, and even at Harvard Divinity School, he had wandered and struggled, wanting to be himself, but also trying to prove he could keep up with the crowd. Through it all he was a social idealist, deeply influenced by William Sloane Coffin, then chaplain at Yale, and Harvey Cox at Harvard. He had spent one Holy Week fasting with fellow divinity school students in the Washington, D.C. jail, protesting the tragedy of the Vietnam War. After graduation he had been a case worker on the staffs of Senator James Abourezk and later Senator George McGovern, spending much of his time dealing with the problems of the Native American in western South Dakota. Over the years there had been a couple of encounters with police over drinking episodes.

There was that early Saturday morning in Sioux Falls when Randy insisted we must talk. This would not be an easy visit he said. He had spent most of the night in jail after being picked up on a DWI charge, in the ditch with an open bottle coming home from a party. He had used the one call he was allowed to get in touch with an attorney friend who had gotten him out on bail. Now he was miserably guilty. "What will the old 'biddies' down at the church say about this when they read it in the paper tonight?" Even though I was disappointed and hurt, I found myself saying, "That's their problem, not ours, Randy, because you're my son." Surely words given me by the Spirit. And the tears flowed as father and son embraced. The competition and misunderstanding of the years began to be washed away in these moments of grace and healing. It was the beginning of a growing friendship between strong-willed men. "Once my child, now my friend."

It was the "old biddies" who offered Randy the first and warmest words of support. One letter in particular stands out. It came from Mrs. Floy Van Ausdall, a strong, longtime member of the church. "We're with you, Randy. We all make mistakes. I know you'll learn and grow from this experience. You have so much to give." What a gift of grace when a church becomes a company of love and encouragement rather than a place of criticism and legalism.

So now after the years of seeking and struggle, this phone call had come! In the months that followed, Randy found spiritual nourishment through a Mennonite Bible study group and a Catholic charismatic prayer group in Rapid City. The Lord always provides!

Then eventually he began to discover where he "fit" while serving three small, rural churches—Hermosa, Keystone, and Fairburn, under the tutelage of Dick Ward, the remarkable pastor of First United Methodist in Rapid City, South Dakota. And what an amazingly diverse congregation came to participate in his ordination—politicians, ranchers, Indians, and all the rest of us.

Now Randy and his talented wife, Elaine—another beautiful gift—are having the time of their lives serving the First Baptist Church of Brookings, a state university town. This is a church that once almost gave up in discouragement, but is now experiencing new life as the fresh winds of the Spirit blow through old, musty places. As Joel, their five-year-old son, says, "That's Jesus' church. My daddy works there."

The power for that ministry flows out of Randy's continuing joyful capitulation to the Lord. In that act of surrender I have seen afresh there is no freedom, no joy, no harvest unless I too continue to live in glad surrender to Him.

Jesus stated it so forthrightly hours before His own death when the Greeks came seeking Him. "Truly, truly, I say to you, unless a grain of wheat falls into the ground and dies, it remains alone; but if it dies, it bears much fruit" (John 12:24). That was the theme and purpose of His whole life.

And the Apostle Paul, using the language of death and resurrection, wrote, "I have been crucified with Christ; it is no longer I who live, but Christ who lives in me" (Galatians 2:20a).

And that sensitive Scotsman, George Matheson, penned strong words that were set to music:

Make me a captive, Lord,
And then I shall be free;
Force me to render up my sword,
And I shall conqueror be.

My will is not my own
Till Thou has made it Thine;
If it would reach a monarch's throne
It must its crown resign.[1]

Yes, I know all that. But will I capitulate, really offer up my sword? That is the heart of the matter. I may tell myself I have my own life to live, and somehow or other I have to make it. That can so easily become my determining motivation, more often than I care to admit. That old, ugly, unbroken self-centeredness can leak out in all kinds of subtle ways. Subconsciously I argue that, I am the senior pastor, why shouldn't I have another raise in salary and get those perks? After all, I carry more responsibility than anyone else on the staff. And is it wrong to find all those gracious comments about my preaching satisfying? Or to be at the head of the line or seated at the speaker's table?

Deep down I must admit that I enjoy being with people of influence and means. Can't they do the kingdom a great deal more good than the poor, troubled people with whom we deal all the time? And I know I shouldn't be so anxious about our growth in membership and giving, but I do want "my" church to advance. I really wanted to attend my son's Little League game, but I had that important board meeting to attend. And I wish my wife wouldn't keep reminding me, even if she does so gently, that I should take my day off each week as well as my whole vacation. I wish she would understand that I have so much to do.

So I keep straining and pushing to get it all done. And I am at the center of so much of it, often pulled in all directions, distracted and frustrated, no longer knowing the joy of the Lord. That freshness which once flowed out of my life like a living stream has dried up. I have run out of gas. My ambition and natural ability and hard work have all been spent. Now I can become discouraged, spiritually neutralized, open to every ill wind that blows—apathy, sexual lust, anger, cynicism, and temptation of every sort. A candidate for burnout, if not dropout!

But the One who first called has not given up on me! His voice is like the crowing of a rooster in the early morning while I am trying to warm my hands at an alien fire. He keeps pursuing, calling, nudging, reminding, sometimes banging me over the head to get my attention.

How gracious of Him to let me hear that sharp reminder. Now I am ashamed, willing to seek His forgiveness, again to submit to His Lordship and confess that I do love Him "more than these." "For the Lord disciplines him whom He loves" (Hebrews 12:6).

So experiences of helplessness and humiliation have often been times of surrender and renewal, as when I left the worship service in pain, knowing I had come unprepared that day to feed the people spiritually when they were hungering for a word from the Lord. Or when I was given a kind, but firm, word of correction by one of our church leaders, "It might be better, Pastor, at the next business meeting if you didn't say anything. Then the people could speak their minds more freely." Or finding myself flat on my back in the cardiac unit discovering I had a badly blocked artery, on my birthday of all days, when most of the family had come home to celebrate. Helpless, dependent, discovering existentially how fragile life is, when I had falsely assumed I was almost indestructible physically. Grateful for the disciplined, caring physician and nurses who helped me through an angioplasty which opened the artery again. Able to go home after a few days with a new respect for the "temple" the Lord had given me to live in, submitting to a new diet including skim milk, oatmeal, fish, and fruit after years of enjoying too much rich Scandinavian food. (Lutefisk is low in dissolved fats, however.)

Then some months later I found myself standing helplessly at my beloved wife's bedside on a Saturday night desperately hoping the doctor would show up. Ruth was struggling for every breath in the grip of a vicious asthma attack which had gone on for several days. Her breathing was so shallow and the inhalation treatments did not seem to be giving her any relief. Then I heard her whisper, "I'm so tired. It's all right if I go." I realized then how much I really loved this precious woman who had been my companion and friend and lover for forty-four years! And I knew that I had often taken her for granted, even neglected her, not understanding how dangerous and debilitating her asthma had been now for all these years. And she had been unselfish and affirming all through the years—gentle, loving Ruth.

I could only surrender to her anew, remembering that husbands are to love their wives "as Christ loved the church and gave Himself up for her" (Ephesians 5:25). An incredible assignment! Once again I silently renewed my commitment to her, there by the bedside, vowing that I would seek to care for her with that kind of love. But that night I also gave my life anew to the One who holds all our times and conditions in His hands.

It was then the doctor came, a kind, believing man, truly an answer to prayer! He was ordering a change in medication. Yes, he knew things were "a bit rough" but he was certain Ruth would come out of this.

Then a peace came, and little by little so did healing. After thirteen long days, when I was able to take Ruth home, I was a chastened, humbled, grateful man! I had learned anew that His grace and power can only come through a yielded life!

But there are also those wondrous times when I have been overwhelmed by the richness of a grace I do not deserve. . . . Hearing "There Is a Fountain Filled with Blood" being played softly during the serving of the cup at the Lord's Supper. . . . Realizing afresh that at best I am only a forgiven sinner who has tasted of God's forgiving love. . . . Or hearing our eager, outgoing daughter, Miriam, tenderly close a telephone conversation, "I love you, Dadso." Or that precious moment when Elizabeth, our oldest granddaughter, threw her arms around my neck and tearfully cried out, "I'm so happy, Grandpa," just after being baptized. The list goes on and on, "from grace to grace"—being forgiven by a fellow member I have offended; or the air being filled with the throbbing, thrilling song of a meadowlark in the early morning as Ruth and I are walking; or that wondering, hope-filled question raised by Karen Schirer after we had prayed together, "Is that what it means to be born again?"

Once again I am brought back in praise and thanksgiving to the Source of all our blessings. All I can do now is capitulate, fall on my knees before this Extravagant Giver and cry out, "My Lord and my God!"

It is only in this posture—the kneeling, open, repentant, expectant spirit—we can receive our Lord's greatest gift—the intimacy of Himself! The Spirit of the Resurrected Christ! The Holy Spirit! This is the Paraclete, the One who runs alongside encouraging us, promised to those who would wait and dare believe. Then He fills, baptizes, immerses us in His own life. He is the One who then guides, teaches, and empowers us to be His witnesses. Now we bear the fruits of the Spirit—love, joy, peace, patience, and all the rest, becoming Christlike. And are gifted for His mission, filled with love for one another, but also for the loveless and unwanted.

It is not a question of how much of the Holy Spirit we have, but how much of us the Holy Spirit has!

It is only when this Spirit is given to God's people that we are willing to submit to one another out of reverence for Christ. Then we begin to live as members of one another, to share one another's burdens, to serve one another as we weep and laugh together in the harmony of Christ.

How clearly I saw this the day Doug and Dalene Johnson came slowly walking forward to join the church accompanying Doug's father and mother, Howard and Alice. Howard was a living miracle after suffering a massive aneurysm at the base of his skull and spending eight months in Wesley Hospital. It was not only the skilled care of the hospital staff, but the stubborn, gentle love of Alice, supported by their son Doug, and the prayers of God's people that literally "called" him back to life.

Howard and Alice, a beautiful pastoral couple, had come to Wichita to retire where their son, Doug, was practicing law. Howard had been struck down a few days after arriving!

The day finally came when I was asked to verify Howard's ordination so he could marry Doug and Dalene in a small family wedding in their apartment. His certificate of ordination had gotten misplaced in the move.

Now here they were — all four of them — coming to join this spiritual family, Doug gently guiding his father to the front. It was a tender moment, a living picture of what was happening to us at Second and Broadway. For more and more of us were sharing our strengths and weaknesses, submitting to one another in the Spirit of Christ. And the Johnsons entered quickly and enthusiastically into the new thing the Lord was doing among us. They were willing to accept any responsibility — in leadership or lowly service to the glory of God. This had a contagious effect on our whole congregation.

There came a day when I knew in my heart, painful as it was, that our ministry in Wichita was drawing to a close. Once again Ruth understood that long before I did. Again I resisted! After all I was only sixty-six and in excellent health. I loved my work, the rhythm and the challenge of it, the preaching and the calling, the pull and the lift of the congregation—all of it—and even managed to struggle with the administration of it reasonably well. And how could I leave that gifted, supportive staff which had been so carefully drawn together? That loving team committed to Christ and His people and one another. Perhaps I could go on until I was seventy, I told myself.

But there was a deeper voice. What was best for these beloved people at this time? This was the Lord's church, not mine. On long walks at Lobster Lake that summer Ruth and I searched our hearts and prayed about all this, asking what did the Lord really want. As we journeyed home in August of 1986, I knew what I had to do. So I bared my heart to some of our key leaders that first Saturday we were home. There were questions, but they understood. When Roger Fraley asked if I was seeking their counsel or had already made up my mind, I could only answer that as far as I understood the Lord's will the decision had been made.

I came to the worship service the next day with a strange mixture of pain and peace. How do you tell people you love that this chapter of our life together is coming to an end? That the Lord was leading us into a new adventure, most often called retirement? But how can one ever withdraw from the Lord's ministry? Joel, our younger son, phrased it beautifully in a song he wrote for a Godspeed celebration some months later, "And now it's time for new seeds to be sown."

At the close of the worship that Sunday I spoke to these people as trusted friends, truly sisters and brothers. Our first and deepest concern was for the spiritual welfare of the church, which is the Lord's, not ours, We had been privileged to lead the church through an era which was now ending. We could only praise the Lord together for what we had seen Him do. And at this stage in our lives Ruth and I wanted to spend more time with each other and with our children and their families. Then we had invitations from churches longing for renewal and hoped we could respond to some of these invitations.

So this was a time of release, of letting go. Easter Sunday, eight months away, would be our last Sunday, the Lord willing. These months could be an exhilarating time of growth and reaching out for Christ rather than hanging crepe. Would the people affirm us in this and send us off with their blessing and prayers? If so, were they willing to stand? There was a hushed pause, some tears, then our church moderator, Jim Wilson, stood. Then others, here and there, until all were standing. It was confirmation of our decision and our next step. Like Randy, it was for me capitulation to a larger will than my own.

So we left! There was a glorious party "celebrating our times together." A weekend of laughter and music, of affirmation and worship, a time of praising God for all He had done and would continue to do. And it had all been quietly engineered by Dalene Johnson and scores of people in league with my secretary, LeeDel. A gracious statement of love, distributed at the Friday night banquet at Beech Activity Center, read in part, "Moreover, because of what Christ has done, we have become gifts to God that He delights in, for as part of God's sovereign plan we were chosen from the beginning to be His and all things happen just as He decided long ago" (Ephesians 1:11-12, TLB). And it went on to read, "We have laughed together, cried together, learned together, and worked together. It is beautiful to realize that we are only beginning our eternal lives together." It was signed "Your Forever Family."

And so Ruth and I moved into the next chapter of our life in Christ—sowing new seeds for Him! But we left wondering, hoping, praying—perhaps with some "fleshly anxiety." What would happen now? Had we built on gold, silver, and precious stones, or on wood, hay, and stubble? Had we allowed the Lord to build the church or had this been too much "Fredrikson's church"? Would the ministries launched during these twelve years fade and die because they were my ideas or flourish and grow because they were the Lord's doing?

There can be lack of continuity, a zig-zag in ministry, even a starting and stopping, in congregational life as pastors come and go. Each with his own style and favorite programs. So every "pastoral era" becomes a chapter in itself with little if any relation to the one who came before and no preparation for the one who comes after. In the end the church can become confused and disheartened.

But it need not be that way. A pastor can come to a congregation grateful for all that has gone before, eager to serve, knowing it is the Lord who gives the increase whether he plants or waters. His calling is to encourage and equip the laity—the people of God—that they may discover their gifts and find their place of ministry. Then the body will be truly built up and the way will be prepared for the next "fellow worker." So we left praying a foundation had been laid on which some other pastor could build.

Of course, there was a time of readjustment and uncertainty among the people. But we shall be everlastingly grateful to that core of faithful, committed lay people who held things together and moved forward knowing this was the Lord's work. Like Aquila and Priscilla, they had been called into places of responsibility which they did not shirk. Time invested in one-on-one discipling, in small Bible study and prayer groups, and in on-the-job training now bore fruit. And the church came through a year of some staff changes and four very different interim pastors strengthened and expectant.

A carefully selected search committee was finally led to call a gifted, younger man as senior pastor. Vic Gordon, who had been chaplain at Wheaton College for six years following five years at Sioux Falls College, is a gifted teacher, an eloquent expositor of God's Word, a lover of people, who has a vision and a passion for what the church is called to be! He and Sue, with their four children and even their boxer, Hershiser, have brought all kinds of life and excitement to the congregation. We have a warm, supportive relationship which is truly a blessing. I rejoice in all his victories!

And the ministry to the poor and homeless continues, led now by Ralph Sanderson. Meals are now served to the hungry on Thursdays. The Tuesday noon Bible study, coordinated by Dick Coe, still ministers to hundreds of downtown people. San and Sineerat Jittawait continue to pastor the internationals and are now reaching a new generation of college students from overseas. And more and more visitors are coming to worship, drawn by the presence of Christ among the people.

The life and ministry of First Baptist has been sharpened and clarified by a vision statement. Discussed and prayed over and "hammered out" over eight months under the sensitive, faithful leadership of Wyatt Hoch, it was adopted by the congregation and declares in part:

> We have been gathered here by an act of God to serve Him. We have sought, and continue to seek, His will for us.... We trust the Holy Spirit to help us live out this vision in our life together.... We commit ourselves to unconditionally love, nurture, and care for one another as brothers and sisters bonded by Christ's love.... We pledge our time and resources to meet the physical, emotional, and spiritual needs of people, and to further peace and justice in the world. God has given us a unique opportunity to pursue His Kingdom among one another, our families, the greater Wichita area, and the world, in cooperation with American Baptists and all other Christians. We offer ourselves to Him in that pursuit. To God be the Glory.

So the church at Second and Broadway will not die, for it is Christ's and not ours! He bought it with His own precious blood and He is the one who builds it through the obedience of those who confess His name. "And the powers of death shall not prevail against it" (Matthew 16:18).

Notes

Chapter One
Catherine Marshall, *Something More* (Carmel, New York: Guideposts Associates, Inc., published by arrangement with McGraw-Hill Book Co., Inc., 1974), p. 95.

Chapter Four
Catherine Marshall, *Beyond Ourselves* (New York: McGraw-Hill Book Company, 1961), p. 182.

Chapter Six
G.A. Studdert Kennedy, *Rough Rhymes of a Padre* (New York: George H. Doran Company, 1989), pp. 16–17.

Chapter Eight
George Matheson, *Cantate Domino* (Geneva: World's Student Christian Federation Hymnal, Fifth Edition), p. 76.